best | designed

Martin Nicholas Kunz . Christian Schönwetter

outdoor living

TERRACES . BALCONIES . ROOFTOPS . COURTYARDS
TERRASSEN . BALKONE . DACHTERRASSEN . HÖFE

avedition

content

introduction | in the "intermediate" empire

This book will not interest stay-at-homes. Here, it is about spending time in the fresh air, the book features locations, where you feel good staying outdoors for a few hours or only a brief moment, whether it is at a barbeque on the terrace, a cigarette break on the balcony, or sunbathing on the roof terrace. In short: here, it is about the transition between building and the outdoors.

This transition zone has many facets; at times, it is formed as a veranda, at other times, as a terrace, as a courtyard, atrium or patio, as a balcony, as a loggia or even as a roof terrace. All these different forms have one thing in common: they are constantly oscillating between inside and outside. You are no longer really in the building, but neither are you completely in a garden nor on the street. You are standing between warm and cold, between the private and public sphere, you are both outside and in your own four walls. You are moving in an "Empire of the Intermediate".

These transitory rooms are a relatively recent invention in the history of living. The courtyard alone looks back over several thousands of years, people already lived in atrium houses in ancient Roman colonies. The last chapter of this book looks at modern interpretations of this traditional outdoor space. The history of terrace, balcony and roof terrace, however, which the remaining three chapters of this book are devoted to with up-to-date examples, dates back for a shorter time. Balconies on apartment

buildings first appear in the Biedermeier period, they mainly provided a small space outdoors on the Bel Étage, although they primarily served as decoration for the building. Later, they were incorporated in the building of rental apartments and were meant to give them a representative character. However, they were only really used at the end of the nineteenth century and made a contribution to healthy living in the fresh air. The situation was not much different with terraces and roof gardens.

Only with the rise of the middle class did these outdoor spaces enter into the history of living.

The book provides a broad overview on recent developments in the design of these outdoor spaces, which are next to buildings. Its four chapters attempt to order the variety of architectural examples, which is not always easy, as many buildings either offer their residents several different kinds of places in the open air

or else they explore new avenues in a typological context, which do not fit into recognized categories.

Christian Schönwetter

introduction | im reich des „zwischen"

Dieses Buch ist nichts für Stubenhocker. Hier geht es um den Aufenthalt an der frischen Luft, hier geht es um Orte, an denen man sich ein paar Stunden oder auch nur einen kurzen Augenblick unter freiem Himmel wohl fühlt, sei es bei einem Grillabend auf der Terrasse, einer Zigarettenpause auf dem Balkon oder einem Sonnenbad auf der Dachterrasse. Kurz: Hier geht es um den Schwellenbereich zwischen Gebäude und Außenraum.

Diese Übergangszone kennt viele Facetten; mal ist sie als Veranda ausgebildet, mal als Terrasse, als Hof, Atrium oder Patio, als Balkon, als Loggia oder aber als Dachgarten. Eines ist allen diesen Erscheinungsformen gemein: Sie oszillieren beständig zwischen innen und außen. Man befindet sich nicht mehr richtig im Gebäude, aber auch noch nicht komplett im Garten oder auf der Straße. Man steht zwischen warm und kalt, zwischen privater und öffentlicher Sphäre, ist gleichzeitig draußen und

in den eigenen vier Wänden. Man bewegt sich in einem Reich des „Zwischen".

Diese Schwellenräume sind eine relativ junge Erfindung in der Geschichte des Wohnens. Lediglich der Hof blickt auf mehrere Jahrtausende zurück, schon in altrömischen Kolonien lebten die Menschen in Atriumhäusern. Das letzte Kapitel dieses Buches beschäftigt sich mit modernen Interpretationen dieses traditionsreichen Außenraums. Die Geschichte von Terrasse, Balkon und Dachterrasse jedoch,

denen sich die übrigen drei Kapitel des Buches mit aktuellen Beispielen widmen, reicht weniger weit zurück. Balkone an Wohngebäuden etwa tauchen erst im Biedermeier auf. Meist boten sie auf der Beletage einen kleinen Austritt, dienten jedoch in erster Linie zur Zierde des Gebäudes. Später hielten sie auch Einzug im Mietshausbau, dem sie einen repräsentativeren Charakter verleihen sollten. Doch erst ab dem Ende des 19. Jahrhunderts wurden sie wirklich genutzt und leisteten einen Beitrag zum

gesunden Wohnen an der frischen Luft. Mit Terrassen und Dachgärten verhielt es sich nicht viel anders. Erst mit einem erstarkten Bürgertum fanden diese Außenräume Eingang in die Geschichte des Wohnens.

Das Buch gibt einen breiten Überblick über gegenwärtige Entwicklungen bei der Gestaltung dieser gebäudenahen Freiräume. Seine vier Kapitel versuchen die Vielfalt der Architekturbeispiele zu ordnen, was nicht immer einfach ist, da viele Bauten entweder

ihren Bewohnern mehrere Arten von Orten im Freien bieten oder aber typologisch neue Wege beschreiten, die sich einer Einordnung in bekannte Kategorien entziehen.

Christian Schönwetter

terraces

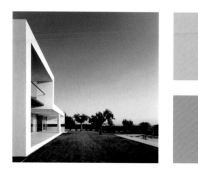

casa CH | barcelona . spain

DESIGN: BAAS Jordi Badia + Mercè Sangenís

The architects describe a detached house, which they erected at Barcelona's city limits, as a matchbox that has fallen onto the lawn. It stands as a gleaming white building on the site, secluded from the neighboring houses and opening towards the garden. The glass façade on this side recedes to the building's interior, as though somebody pushed the matchbox drawer in. A terrace with a roof is created and the windows are shielded from too much direct sunlight. The key: when the residents want to use their outdoor space completely undisturbed and to stop anyone looking in from the outside, they can draw a curtain, which runs around the outer edge of the terrace and, of course, also serves as a source of shade. A horizontal slit in the exterior wall, which runs at eye level when you are seated, enables you to take secret glances to the outside.

Als Streichholzschachtel, die auf den Rasen gefallen ist, beschreiben die Architekten ein Wohnhaus, das sie am Stadtrand von Barcelona errichteten. Strahlend weiß sitzt es auf dem Grundstück, verschließt sich zur Nachbarbebauung und öffnet sich zum Garten. An dieser Seite zieht sich die Glasfassade ins Innere des Baukörpers zurück, als habe man die Schublade in die Streichholzschachtel hineingeschoben. Dadurch entsteht eine überdachte Terrasse und die Fenster sind vor zu viel direkter Sonneneinstrahlung geschützt. Der Clou: Wenn die Bewohner ihren Freisitz völlig ungestört nutzen und jeglichen Einblick von außen verhindern wollen, können sie einen Vorhang zuziehen, der an der äußeren Kante der Terrasse verläuft und nebenbei natürlich auch als Schattenspender dient. Ein horizontaler Schlitz in der Außenwand, der, wenn man sitzt, auf Augenhöhe verläuft, erlaubt gleichzeitig heimliche Blicke nach außen.

haus im gässele | günzburg-reisensburg . germany
D E S I G N : biehler-weith associated, building-design-projects

The backbone of a detached house in Günzburg is formed by a man-high wall section, which extends over the entire length of the site. It begins at a small forecourt as a boundary wall to the neighbor, then it becomes part of the building that forms the rear wall of the living room; it carries the upper floor and continues in the garden behind the house, in order to protect the terrace from neighbours' inquisitive looks. The outdoor seating is connected by the wall to the interior space, which is only separated from the exterior by a frameless window. It ends at a pool. This runs sideways along the wall and is fed by a wide stream of water and forms the rear end of the terrace. The material of the screen, a light, French limestone is also used for the floor in the open-air seating area. The residents, a retired couple, also have a balcony and a gravel courtyard available for outdoor life.

Eine mannshohe Wandscheibe über die gesamte Grundstückslänge bildet das Rückgrat eines Einfamilienhauses in Günzburg. Sie beginnt an einem kleinen Vorplatz als Grenzmauer zum Nachbarn, wird dann zu einem Teil des Gebäudes, der die Rückwand des Wohnzimmers bildet und das Obergeschoss trägt, und setzt sich hinter dem Haus in den Garten fort, um dort die Terrasse vor neugierigen Blicken der Nachbarn zu schützen. Der Sitzplatz im Freien wird von ihr an den Innenraum gebunden, der nur durch eine rahmenlose Verglasung vom Außenraum getrennt ist. Sie endet an einem Becken. Es läuft seitlich an ihr entlang, wird von einem breiten Wasserschwall gespeist und bildet den hinteren Abschluss der Terrasse. Das Material der Scheibe, ein heller französischer Kalkstein, liegt auch am Boden des Freibereichs. Für das Leben im Freien stehen den Bewohnern, einem Ehepaar im Ruhestand, zusätzlich ein Balkon und ein kiesbedeckter Hof zur Verfügung.

casa tagomago | san carlos, ibiza . spain
DESIGN: Carlos Ferrater

A luxurious holiday home is located on a slightly sloping plot in north eastern Ibiza. Its interior and exterior organization is interlocked in a particular way: the bedrooms are arranged along a long, extended axis and are separated from each other by small open-plan areas. Once the visitor has passed the row of these intimate, individual rooms, the axis finally ends in the central and common living room. The main terrace is situated in front of this room with a view of the sea and the island of Tagomago. A large Bris soleil of light concrete, which stands as an independent structure in front of the building, gives shade and a roof section over part of the terrace. The light natural stone of the boundary wall is in large-size stonework and forms a contrast to the warm brown tone of the mostly dry earth, on which very little grows apart from pine and cypress trees.

Auf leicht abfallendem Gelände im Nordosten Ibizas liegt ein luxuriöses Ferienhaus. Seine Organisation verzahnt innen und außen auf besondere Weise: Die Schlafräume ordnen sich entlang einer lang gestreckten Achse und werden von kleinen Freibereichen voneinander getrennt. Hat der Besucher die Reihe dieser intimen Individualräume passiert, mündet die Achse schließlich in den zentralen gemeinschaftlichen Wohnraum. Vor diesem liegt die Hauptterrasse mit Aussicht auf das Meer und die Insel Tagomago. Ein großer Brisesoleil aus hellem Beton, der als eigenständige Struktur vor dem Bauwerk steht, spendet Schatten und überdacht einen Teil der Terrasse. Der helle Naturstein ihrer Umfassungswand, großformatig verarbeitet, bildet einen Kontrast zu dem warmen Braun der meist trockenen Erde, auf der außer Pinien und Zedern nicht viel wächst.

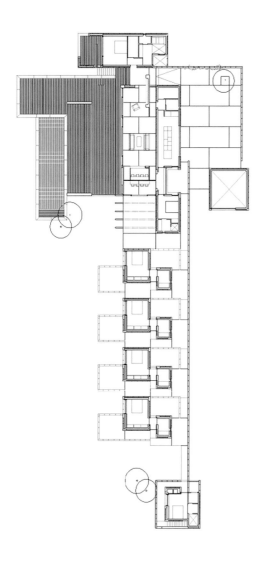

hameau de gîtes ruraux | jupilles . france
DESIGN: Edouard Francois

A holiday home site in Jupilles explores the boundaries between nature and architecture. Inspired by the location directly at the forest-edge and the imposing, century-old trees, the architect attempted to use the vegetation for the design. Each one of the ten holiday homes is a small box, which disappears behind a row of plants with exactly the same height as the building. Window openings are cut out of this green layer, exactly as in a normal façade. The plants adopt the cubed shape of the building and also continue this shape in the external space; they grow so tightly together and are cut in such a way as to look like an enclosed cuboid. The terrace, which is situated next to each house, therefore appears like an interior space cut out of the green mass. The inhabitable parcels of vegetation are freely distributed around the site, where the grass is not cut, to allow a meadow to grow naturally. The holiday homes can only be distinguished from the forest with some difficulty.

Die Grenzen zwischen Natur und Architektur lotet eine Ferienhausanlage in Jupilles aus. Durch die Lage direkt am Waldrand und die imposanten hundert Jahre alten Bäume inspiriert, versuchte der Architekt, die Vegetation für den Entwurf nutzbar zu machen. Jedes der zehn Ferienhäuser ist eine kleine Box, die hinter einer Reihe Pflanzen verschwindet, welche exakt die gleiche Höhe wie das Gebäude hat. Fensteröffnungen sind aus dieser grünen Schicht wie aus einer normalen Fassade herausgeschnitten. Die Pflanzen nehmen die Kubatur des Gebäudes auf und setzen sie auch im Außenraum fort; sie stehen so dicht beisammen und werden so beschnitten, dass sie wie ein geschlossener Quader wirken. Die Terrasse, die neben jedem Haus liegt, erscheint daher wie ein Innenraum, der aus dem grünen Volumen ausgeschnitten ist. Frei verteilt stehen die bewohnbaren Vegetationspakete auf dem Grundstück, das nicht gemäht wird, um eine natürliche Wiese wachsen zu lassen. Nur schwer sind die Ferienhäuser vom Wald zu unterscheiden.

haus p. | ranggen . austria
DESIGN: Erich Gutmorgeth

Erich Gutmorgeth's speciality is difficult locations. The architect advises his client to find a site that nobody else wants to obtain, because these plots are mostly available at a low price. Then, the saved money is meant to improve the building. A detached home near Innsbruck shows the result, which can be achieved with this strategy: here, the view had to be shielded from the mundane, neighboring structure in country house style. Gutmorgeth therefore covered the house with a second skin of perpendicular slats, set apart from the façade at a small distance and creating an intermediate zone, which is used as a terrace. The terrace extends over two floors up to the roof, so that it is both protected from rain and appears particularly spacious. The external layer filters the view towards the outside: if the resident looks through the façade vertically, the surroundings become visible, but if he directs his gaze at a tangent across the slats, they close and block out the neighboring area. The second skin breaks up in some places and allows well-calculated views of the charming Tirolian hills in the distance.

Schwierige Grundstücke sind die Spezialität von Erich Gutmorgeth. Der Architekt rät seinen Bauherren, sich ein Gelände zu suchen, das sonst niemand haben will, weil diese meist günstig zu bekommen sind. Das eingesparte Geld soll dann dem Gebäude zugute kommen. In der Nähe von Innsbruck zeigt ein Einfamilienhaus, welches Ergebnis sich mit dieser Strategie erreichen lässt. Hier musste der Blick auf die banale Nachbarbebauung im Landhausstil abgeschirmt werden. Gutmorgeth überzog das Haus deshalb mit einer zweiten Haut aus senkrechten Latten, die mit einigem Abstand vor der Fassade verlaufen und einen Zwischenbereich schaffen, der als Terrasse genutzt wird. Diese Terrasse reicht über zwei Geschosse bis unter das Dach, so dass sie sowohl vor Regen geschützt ist als auch besonders großzügig wirkt. Die äußere Schicht filtert den Ausblick: Schaut ein Bewohner senkrecht durch sie hindurch, wird die Umgebung sichtbar, lässt er den Blick dagegen tangential über die Latten streifen, schließen sie sich und blenden die Nachbarschaft aus. An einigen Stellen reißt diese zweite Haut auf und gewährt wohlkalkulierte Ausblicke auf die reizvollen Tiroler Berge in der Ferne.

wohnhaus schlüter | karlsruhe . germany

DESIGN: Meixner Schlüter Wendt Architekten + Walter Ziser

A residential area in Karlsruhe makes it possible to live right in the middle of the forest, since the houses in the "Waldstadt" ("Forest City") district are built between the trees of an old pine forest. To create an intense relationship between building and this special environment, the architects who designed Haus Schlüter decided to construct their building on the site, similar to a monolithic structure, to cut different volumes out of it and, in this way, to allow the external space to penetrate the building. The empty spaces that were created in the process became a terrace, loggia and entrance area. The color scheme and material selection make the idea visible. While the outsides of the structure are painted dark, all interventions are in a white tone. The subtractive principle of cutting smaller pieces out of a large mass creates open spaces under a roof cover that protects from rain and too much sun. The roof cover allows the low, winter sun to shine into the living room, but provides shade in the summer and allows fewer rays into the house, so dispensing with a need for sunshade and air conditioning.

Mitten im Wald zu wohnen ermöglicht eine Siedlung in Karlsruhe, denn die Häuser des Quartiers „Waldstadt" sind zwischen die Bäume eines alten Kiefernwaldes gebaut. Um eine intensive Beziehung zwischen Gebäude und dieser besonderen Umgebung herzustellen, entschieden sich die Architekten des Hauses Schlüter, ihren Bau einem Monolithen gleich auf das Grundstück zu setzen, verschiedene Volumina aus ihm herauszuschneiden und auf diese Weise den Außenraum ins Gebäude eindringen zu lassen. Die entstandenen Leerräume werden zu Terrasse, Loggia und Eingangsbereich. Farbgestaltung und Materialwahl veranschaulichen das Konzept. Während die Außenseiten des Baukörpers dunkel gefärbt sind, tragen alle Einschnitte einen weißen Anstrich. Das subtraktive Prinzip, aus einer großen Masse kleinere Stücke herauszuschneiden, schafft überdachte Freiräume, die vor Regen und zu viel Sonne schützen. Der Dachüberstand lässt die niedrige Wintersonne tief in den Wohnraum scheinen, im Sommer dagegen spendet er Schatten und lässt weniger Strahlen ins Haus, so dass auf Sonnenschutz und Kühlung verzichtet werden konnte.

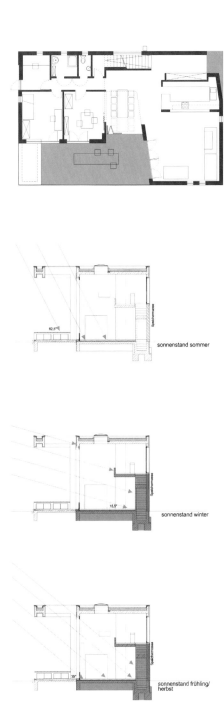

sonnenstand sommer

sonnenstand winter

sonnenstand frühling/
herbst

garten haus zum delphin | zürich . switzerland

DESIGN: Nägeliarchitekten Walter Nägeli Gudrun Sack

High above the lake and town center, a 1920s banker's villa is located on a steep slope. The garden area, which also dates from this period, is gradually being redesigned. It consists of several parts: a pergola, a tea house, several fountains, a cast-iron path, a handmade, geometrical and intricate "stone carpet", new planting and a terrace extension. The goal of the redesigning work is to connect the building more closely to the garden and the surrounding landscape, that is, the mountains in the distance. A terrace with a newly erected pergola, among others, is to achieve this effect. This structure is an interior in an exterior space, which is formed by a series of artificial, "woven trees". Depending on the season, it appears either more open or closed through its leafy state; in winter, the woven shape is slightly reminiscent of an Arabian pattern, because it also filters and transforms the light in a special way. It consists of conical-shaped, cedar wood slats, which were fixed together by hand in a complex, geometrical structure at a workshop near Berlin. It was then transported in low-loading trucks to Zurich. As the cedar wood is preserved in its natural condition, it can gradually age. The floor of the intricately designed external space is covered by sand-colored areas of gravel, bordered by a frame of broken Maggia gneiss.

Hoch über dem See und der Innenstadt liegt an einem steilen Hang eine Bankiersvilla aus den zwanziger Jahren. Die Gartenanlage, die ebenfalls aus dieser Zeit stammt, wird nach und nach umgestaltet. Sie besteht aus mehreren Teilen: einer Pergola, einem Teehaus, mehreren Brunnen, einem gusseisernen Weg, einem aufwändigen handgearbeiteten „Steinteppich", Neupflanzungen und einer Terrassenerweiterung. Ziel der Umgestaltung ist es, das Gebäude enger mit dem Garten und der umgebenden Landschaft, den Bergen in der Ferne, zu verbinden. Hierzu dient unter anderem eine Terrasse mit einer neu errichteten Pergola, ein Innenraum im Außenraum, der sich aus einer Reihe künstlicher „geflochtener Bäume" zusammensetzt. Durch seine Berankung erscheint dieser Bereich je nach Jahreszeit offener oder geschlossener; im Winter erinnert das Geflecht ein wenig an arabische Muster, auch weil es das Licht auf besondere Weise filtert und verwandelt. Das Geflecht besteht aus konisch geschnittenen Zedernholzleisten, die nach einer komplexen Geometrie in der Nähe von Berlin von Hand zusammengefügt und anschließend mit Tiefladern nach Zürich transportiert wurden. Da das Zedernholz naturbelassen ist, kann es allmählich altern. Den Boden des aufwändig gestalteten Außenraums bedecken sandfarbene Kiesfelder, eingefasst von Rahmen aus gebrochenem Maggia-Gneis.

SPS einfamilienhaus | vienna . austria
DESIGN: querkraft

Anybody who wants to build a real, detached house right in the center of an allotment colony has to think of something special, so as not to contravene existing planning regulations. This is what happened at Wilhelminenberg in Vienna's sixteenth district. In these allotment areas, building is limited to a base of 50 m² and to avoid these regulations, the architects divided the sloping plot of land into three parcels, only to reintegrate the building segments with one each other afterwards. As a result, a basic shape for the structure was created of about 40 meters long and 5 meters wide. This building is buried deep in the slope and opens its southern side onto a garden that is moved up to give a panoramic view over the city. The transition between living space and the raised veranda is fluid and on hot summer days, sliding doors can be opened so that the inside becomes the outside and vice versa. A steel pipe construction covered with ridged, acrylic glass serves as a weather shield and gives the building a rather improvized character, as is usual with arbors—a reference to the location. The owners' weakness for sailing boats is visible in the terrace's surface: planks of oiled, tropical wood were laid like a ship's deck. According to the builder, the wood was tested by Greenpeace and approved as "politically correct".

Wer inmitten einer Kleingartenkolonie ein richtiges Einfamilienhaus errichten will, muss sich schon etwas einfallen lassen, um nicht gegen geltendes Baurecht zu verstoßen. So geschehen am Wilhelminenberg im 16. Wiener Bezirk. Um die Grundflächenbeschränkung von 50 Quadratmetern, wie sie in solchen Siedlungen gefordert wird, zu umgehen, teilten die Architekten das Hanggrundstück in drei Parzellen auf und verkuppelten die Bauteile anschließend miteinander. Daraus resultiert die Grundform des rund 40 Meter langen und 5 Meter breiten Baukörpers. Dieser gräbt sich tief in die Böschung ein und öffnet seine Südseite einem vorgelagerten Garten mit Panoramablick über die Stadt. Der Übergang zwischen Wohnraum und aufgeschütteter Veranda ist fließend, an heißen Sommertagen lassen geöffnete Schiebetüren innen zu außen werden und umgekehrt. Eine mit Wellacrylglas bedeckte Stahlrohrkonstruktion dient als Wetterschutz und verleiht dem Gebäude einen etwas improvisierten Charakter, wie er bei Gartenlauben üblich ist – eine Referenz an den Ort. Das Faible der Auftraggeber für Segelboote zeigt sich am Belag der Terrasse: Wie Schiffsplanken wurden Bohlen aus geöltem Tropenholz verlegt, das laut Bauherr durch Greenpeace geprüft und als „politisch korrekt" eingestuft worden ist.

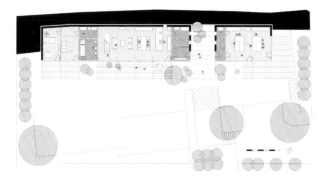

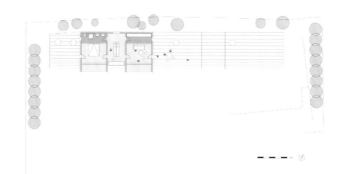

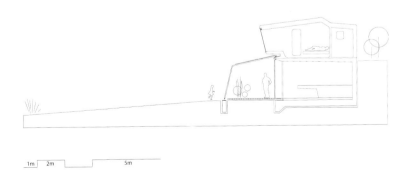

1m | 2m | 5m

haus für eine deutschlehrerin | orsoy . germany

DESIGN: Björn Severin in rheinflügel baukunst

Appropriately, when the architect designed a small, detached house for a German lady teacher, the inspiration was Goethe's Summer House in Weimar. By scaling the arched roof building type, dividing it up and displacing a section, he playfully de-familiarized the structure. This is how a terrace was created, which is framed on two sides and spatially fixed by the displaced building element, which at the same time also provides some shielding from onlookers in the neighborhood. The terrace is the real center of the introverted house, which is also reflected in the design of the façade. While the "uneven edges" are painted white, the outsides of the original structure are a dark color, which applies equally to the roof and walls. The building's outer façades are intended rather as the rear side, as a repelling shell, which is penetrated by smaller windows at irregular intervals and scattered with technical elements like a satellite dish, solar panel and ventilation shafts. In contrast, the façade of the terrace was kept free of disruptive elements and appears markedly more presentable with French windows, the height of the room. In 2004, the building was chosen to be part of the German entry to the Biennale in Venice.

Goethes Gartenhaus in Weimar diente passenderweise als Inspiration, als der Architekt ein kleines Einfamilienhaus für eine Deutschlehrerin entwarf. Indem er jedoch den Walmdachtypus skalierte, aufschnitt und einen Teil verschob, verfremdete er den Baukörper spielerisch. Auf diese Weise entstand eine Terrasse, die auf zwei Seiten gerahmt und von dem verschobenen Bauteil räumlich gefasst wird, der gleichzeitig auch ein wenig vor Einblicken der Nachbarschaft schützt. Die Terrasse ist das eigentliche Zentrum des introvertierten Hauses, was sich auch an der Fassadengestaltung widerspiegelt. Während die „Schnittkanten" weiß gestrichen sind, tragen die Außenseiten des Ursprungskörpers eine dunkle Farbe, die sich über Dach und Wand gleichermaßen zieht. Die äußeren Fassaden des Gebäudes verstehen sich eher als Rückseite, als abweisende Schale, von kleineren Fenstern in unregelmäßiger Anordnung durchstoßen und mit technischen Elementen wie Satellitenschüssel, Solarkollektor und Abluftrohren bestückt. Die Terrassenfassade hingegen wurde von störenden Elementen freigehalten und wirkt durch raumhohe französische Fenster deutlich repräsentativer. Das Bauwerk wurde 2004 als Teil des deutschen Beitrags zur Biennale in Venedig ausgewählt.

villa 13x13 | freistadt . austria

DESIGN: xarchitekten + Arch. P. Reitmayr

The apartment building is located in the Mühlviertel district near to the Czech border. It has been constructed into the hillside in such a way that you gain entry by the upper level, which is largely a closed box that reigns over the completely glazed section of the garden level. The question immediately arises about the light source for the rooms. The answer is quite simple: the light comes from an inner courtyard as an interface between the public ante-room and the private area, which—almost from the inside—provides the entire floor with daylight. While the upper level enables its inhabitants to lead a very introverted life, the lower level ensures maximum openness to the surroundings. A glass strip, the height of the room, lets the inside merge with the outside. The spatial composition of the building as a box, which seems to be suspended above a glass plinth and extends far beyond it, creates a roofed terrace in the lower floor in a most natural and intelligent way. The situation of the rolling glass façade is rather reminiscent of the glass façade on Le Corbusier's Villa Savoye in Paris. The only difference is that the cube in Freistadt is not based on pilots, as required by the master himself, but on a distinctive concrete "X", which also looks like the architects' signature.

Das Wohnhaus steht in der Mühlviertler Hügellandschaft nahe der tschechischen Grenze. Es ist so in den Hang gebaut, dass die Erschließung über das Obergeschoss erfolgt, das als weitgehend geschlossene Kiste über dem vollständig verglasten Gartengeschoss thront. Sofort drängt sich die Frage auf, woher die Räume ihr Licht beziehen. Die Antwort ist einfach: Hinter einem transluzenten Rolltor befindet sich ein Innenhof als Nahtstelle zwischen öffentlichem Vorraum und privatem Bereich, der die Etage tagsüber – quasi von innen heraus – mit Tageslicht versorgt. Während das obere Stockwerk seinen Bewohnern ein sehr introvertiertes Wohnen unter vollständigem Rückzug von der Außenwelt ermöglicht, gewährt das Untergeschoss eine maximale Öffnung zur Umgebung. Ein raumhohes Glasband lässt innen und außen verschmelzen. Die räumliche Komposition des Gebäudes als Box, die über dem Glassockel zu schweben scheint und weit über diesen hinausragt, schafft auf eine selbstverständliche, einleuchtende Weise im unteren Geschoss eine überdachte Terrasse. Ein wenig erinnert die Situation der geschwungenen Glasfassade an Le Corbusiers Villa Savoye bei Paris. Nur ruht der Kubus in Freistadt nicht auf den vom Meister geforderten Piloti, sondern auf einem markanten Beton-X, das gleichsam wie eine Unterschrift der Architekten wirkt.

wohnüberbauung burriweg | zürich . switzerland

D E S I G N : Frank Zierau Dipl. Ing. Architekt BSA SIA + Ryffel & Ryffel

The residential development at the Burriweg is a step into typological new territory by Frank Zierau; he created multi-faceted "free rooms", which are both internal and external rooms at the same time. The architect planned an arbor for each flat, stacking two of them together to form a small tower and moving them from the building, in order not to overshadow the living space too much. Each arbor is designed as a two-storey summer house, which the tenants can furnish and equip individually. It is higher and offers the residents a different view than, for example, from a balcony, which might be directly added onto the building. The tenants from the upper apartments access their summer houses by a small, steel bridge. The towers are made of a fire-proofed, zinc and steel construction, which reaches eleven meters into the sky and is finished with prefabricated wooden elements, which can be replaced if needed. To provide necessary security from any danger of falls, the density of the trellis-like filling elements increases on the balustrade. Smoothly planed larchwood was used, which already has a lively and historical provenance: it comes from the Swiss Pavillion at Expo 2000 in Hanover; Peter Zumthor designed the structure so that the building material could later quickly be recycled. The famous wood has found a new use at Zurich's Burriweg.

Typologisches Neuland beschreitet Frank Zierau mit der Siedlung am Burriweg, er schuf mehrdeutige „Freizimmer", die Innen- und Außenraum zugleich sind. Der Architekt ordnete jeder Wohnung eine eigene Laube zu, stapelte je zwei davon zu einem kleinen Turm und rückte diesen vom Gebäude ab, um die Wohnräume nicht zu sehr zu verschatten. Jede Laube ist als ein zweigeschossiges Gartenzimmer ausgebildet, das die Mieter individuell möblieren und ausstatten können. Sie ist höher und bietet den Bewohnern eine andere Aussicht als etwa ein Balkon, der direkt am Gebäude angebracht wäre. Aus den oberen Wohnungen gelangen die Mieter über eine Stahlbrücke zu ihrer Laube. Die Türme bestehen aus einer feuerverzinkten Stahlkonstruktion, die sich elf Meter in die Höhe streckt und mit vorfabrizierten Holzelementen, die bei Bedarf ausgewechselt werden können, ausgefacht ist. Um die nötige Absturzsicherheit zu gewährleisten, nimmt die Dichte der spalierartigen Füllelemente im Brüstungsbereich zu. Als Material kam Lärchenholz zum Einsatz, das bereits auf eine bewegte Vergangenheit zurückblicken kann. Es stammt vom Schweizer Pavillon auf der Expo 2000 in Hannover. Peter Zumthor hatte diesen so konzipiert, dass sich der Baustoff später möglichst restlos recyceln lassen sollte. Am Züricher Burriweg hat das prominente Holz nun eine neue Verwendung gefunden.

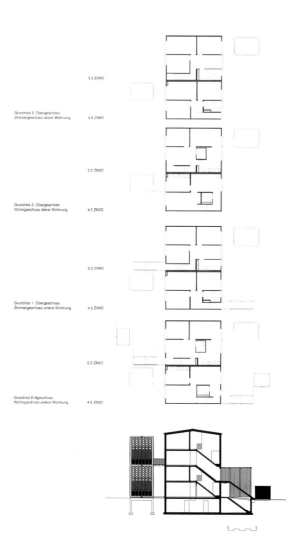

5.5 ZIWO

Grundriss 3. Obergeschoss
Zimmergeschoss obere Wohnung   4.5 ZIWO

5.5 ZIWO

Grundriss 2. Obergeschoss
Wohngeschoss obere Wohnung   4.5 ZIWO

5.5 ZIWO

Grundriss 1. Obergeschoss
Zimmergeschoss untere Wohnung   4.5 ZIWO

5.5 ZIWO

Grundriss Erdgeschoss
Wohngeschoss untere Wohnung   4.5 ZIWO

balconies

illa fleming | barcelona . spain

DESIGN: Jaume Bach

Alteration, change and movement are the central design themes of a residential site in Barcelona. The architect used the balconies, which enclose the building on three sides, for a dual-layered façade. Red plasterwork, interrupted by vertical openings from the floor to the ceiling, forms the inner layer, while the outer layer is formed by mobile, shading elements, which are fixed 60 centimeters in front of the plasterwork façade and consist of an aluminium frame with horizontal wooden slats. Every resident can move these screens horizontally according to his individual needs, so that an arbitrary and constantly changing movement occurs to the overall appearance, depending on the activities of the people throughout the day. The space between the two layers of the façade gets wider in the zone of the living rooms and forms a loggia there, which can be used both as an internal and external room, according to the position of the shading elements. The architects took particular trouble to trap as much light as possible: they had glass panes built in as a balustrade and the wooden floors extend to the outside over the load-bearing concrete support, so that the sun's rays can shine between them and illuminate the balcony situated below. In this way, the exterior, facing side of the balcony panels looks especially narrow, which emphasizes the building's elegant, horizontal line.

Veränderung, Wechsel und Bewegung sind die zentralen gestalterischen Themen einer Wohnanlage in Barcelona. Der Architekt nutzte die Freibereiche, welche die Gebäude auf drei Seiten umschließen, für eine zweischichtige Fassade. Während ein roter Putz, der von vertikalen Öffnungen vom Boden bis zur Decke unterbrochen wird, die innere Schicht darstellt, wird die äußere von beweglichen Verschattungselementen gebildet, die 60 Zentimeter vor der Putzfassade liegen und aus einem Aluminiumrahmen mit horizontalen Holzlamellen bestehen. Jeder Bewohner kann diese Screens nach seinen individuellen Bedürfnissen horizontal verschieben. So entsteht in der Gesamtansicht eine zufällige und ständig wechselnde Bewegung, die von den Aktivitäten der Menschen im Tagesverlauf abhängt. Der Raum zwischen den beiden Fassadenschichten weitet sich im Bereich der Wohnzimmer und bildet dort eine Loggia, die sich sowohl als Innen- wie auch als Außenraum auffassen lässt – je nach Position der Verschattungselemente. Besondere Mühe gaben sich die Architekten, um möglichst viel Licht einzufangen: Als Geländer ließen sie Glasscheiben einbauen und die Holzdielen am Boden ragen nach außen über die tragende Betonplatte hinaus, so dass die Sonnenstrahlen zwischen ihnen hindurch auf den darunter liegenden Balkon scheinen können.

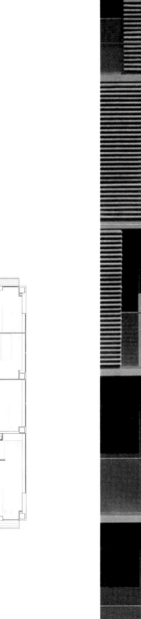

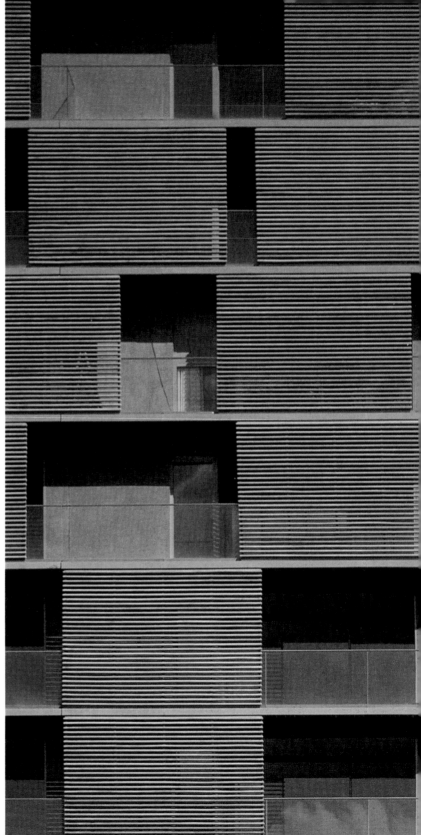

swiss re | munich . germany

DESIGN: BRT Architekten Bothe Richter Teherani + Peter Kluska + Martha Schwartz

The Munich subsidiary of an insurance company treated itself to a balcony of a special kind: it is completed as a suspended hedge. The building consists of a total of 16 wings and is joined together on the upper storeys by a trellis, with climbing plants, and an accessible area. Over a length of 600 meters, the employees can walk around the building in the breezy heights; the steel structure is reached by the maintenance balconies and it also serves as an emergency escape exit. At present, wisteria and Virginia creeper are growing up from the ground level and cover, rather lightly, the wire-netting fence, where they are supposed to flourish and spread out. However, as soon as they have completely enveloped the building, they are cut back as far as the lower edge of the trellis, so that from a distance, the hedge looks as if it is suspended. The architects created a half-transparent layer with the green covering for the building, which rescues employees from the view of a dreary industrial site. Instead, an introverted solution was created, which allows the view from every office to sweep out into a green zone. The American landscape artist, Martha Schwartz, designed the courtyards between the wings. She created a counterpoint to the imposing hedge, dispensed with luscious greenery and worked with water surfaces, gravel and glass splinters.

Einen Balkon der besonderen Art gönnte sich die Münchner Niederlassung einer Versicherungsgesellschaft: Er ist als schwebende Hecke ausgeführt, denn das Gebäude, das aus insgesamt 16 Flügeln besteht, wird in den oberen Geschossen von einem begehbaren Rankgitter zusammengefasst. Auf einer Länge von 600 Metern können die Mitarbeiter hier in luftiger Höhe um das Gebäude herumspazieren. Die Stahlstruktur wird von den Wartungsbalkonen der einzelnen Flügel aus erschlossen und dient im Notfall als Fluchtweg. Momentan wachsen Glyzinien und wilder Wein noch vom Boden empor und bedecken eher spärlich den Maschendrahtzaun, an dem sie in die Breite wuchern sollen. Sobald sie jedoch das Gebäude komplett umschlungen haben, werden sie bis zur Unterkante des Gerüsts entlaubt, so dass die Hecke dann aus der Ferne wirkt, als würde sie schweben. Die Architekten schufen mit der grünen Gebäudehaut eine halbdurchlässige Schicht, die den Mitarbeitern die Aussicht auf ein trostloses Gewerbegebiet erspart. Stattdessen entstand eine introvertierte Lösung, bei welcher der Blick von jedem Büro ins Grüne schweifen kann. Die Höfe zwischen den Flügeln gestaltete die amerikanische Landschaftsarchitektin Martha Schwartz. Sie schuf einen Kontrapunkt zu der gewaltigen Hecke, verzichtete auf üppiges Grün und arbeitete mit Wasserflächen, Kies und Glassplit.

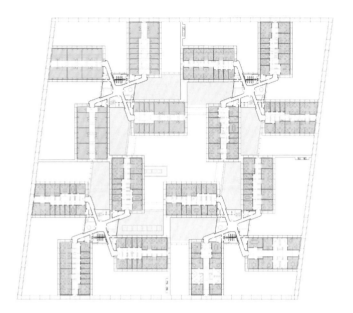

stadthaus wimbergergasse | vienna . austria

DESIGN: Delugan Meissl Associated Architects

A modern interpretation of a classical form: the building fills an empty space in a district full of houses from the turn of the nineteenth century and follows the traditional building structure of the location, where smaller industrial businesses are located behind block-edge development. The new building has space for office units in a courtyard, while apartments face out onto the street. Instead of the typical window bays from the earlier period, they were given a glazed balcony, which is partioned off by a sliding door. The loggias situated in front partially extend over two storeys and because of their unusual height they appear quite spacious, despite a relatively small base. As they are arranged in a strictly modular system, a pattern develops that creates a rhythm to the façade of aluminium and glass. Originally, the external skin was meant to be decorated with planting, but the idea was discarded. Nevertheless, it seems as if the artist, Herwig Kempinger, who was responsible for the design of the façade, has taken up the idea: abstract illustrations of bare trees are printed as a screen-print over the entire glass frontage and provide a sight-screen at balustrade level.

Moderne Interpretation eines klassischen Typus': Das Gebäude schließt eine Baulücke in einem Gründerzeitviertel und folgt dabei der traditionellen Bebauungsstruktur der Umgebung, bei der hinter einem geschlossenen Blockrand kleinere Gewerbebetriebe siedeln. Der Neubau weist Büroeinheiten einen Platz im Hof zu, während Wohnungen zur Straße blicken. Statt der früher üblichen Erker erhielten sie je einen verglasten Balkon, der mittels einer Schiebetür abgetrennt ist. Die vorgelagerten Loggien erstrecken sich teilweise über zwei Geschosse und wirken durch ihre ungewohnte Höhe trotz eher kleiner Grundfläche recht großzügig. Weil sie in einem strikt modularen System angeordnet sind, entsteht ein Muster, das die Fassade aus Aluminium und Glas rhythmisiert. Ursprünglich sollte die Außenhaut begrünt werden, doch der Gedanke wurde verworfen. Dennoch scheint es, als hätte der für die Fassadengestaltung verantwortliche Künstler Herwig Kempinger die Idee aufgegriffen: Abstrahierte Darstellungen von kahlen Bäumen erstrecken sich als Siebdruck über die gesamte Glasfront und dienen im Bereich der Brüstungselemente als Sichtschutz.

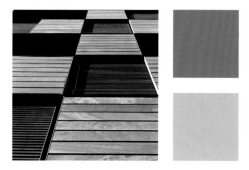

carrer de balmes | barcelona . spain
DESIGN: Carlos Ferrater

The more central the location, the more difficult it is to design outdoor spaces. High prices for land force every square centimeter to be used optimally, so that no space remains for generous balconies. In Barcelona's city center, the architect decided to integrate small loggias towards the street in an apartment and office block. They do not even cut one meter deep into the building, but they offer enough space for a cigarette break any time—in view of the tight space in the urban surroundings, this is still a generous solution. The loggias are part of a finely worked façade composition, which consists of closed and open fields by equal halves, as specified by the regulations in this city district. Four layers, arranged next to each other—on the onion principle—characterize the open-air seating and façade: on the very outer layer, a natural stone cladding, towards the inside, wooden shutters at the height of a single storey, followed by steel railings in the area of the loggias and, behind that, the glass of the balcony doors. This—in fact quite traditional—combination of materials is the same as that of nineteenth century buildings in the neighbourhood, only with a modern interpretation.

Je zentraler die Lage, desto heikler die Gestaltung der Freibereiche. Denn hohe Grundstückspreise zwingen den Architekten dazu, jeden Quadratzentimeter optimal zu nutzen, so dass etwa für üppige Balkone kein Platz bleibt. Bei einem Wohn- und Geschäftshaus in der Stadtmitte von Barcelona entschied sich der Architekt, zur Straße kleine Loggien anzuordnen. Sie schneiden sich nicht einmal einen Meter tief in den Baukörper, bieten aber allemal genug Platz für eine Zigarettenpause – angesichts der Enge des urbanen Umfelds eine immer noch großzügige Lösung. Die Loggien sind Teil einer fein austarierten Fassadenkomposition, die sich je zur Hälfte aus geschlossenen und offenen Feldern zusammensetzt, wie es in diesem Stadtteil vorgeschrieben ist. Vier Schichten, nach dem Zwiebelprinzip hintereinander angeordnet, prägen Freisitze und Fassade: außen eine Natursteinverkleidung, nach innen versetzte geschosshohe Holzfensterläden, gefolgt von Stahlgeländern im Bereich der Loggien und dahinter die Verglasung der Balkontüren. Diese – eigentlich ganz traditionelle – Materialkombination ist die gleiche wie bei den Gründerzeitbauten der Umgebung, jedoch modern interpretiert.

château le lez | montpellier . france
DESIGN: Edouard Francois

The idea of a tree house was the influence when the architect, Eduard Francois, invented a new style of balcony for a residential site in Montpellier: he added an accessible box without a roof in front of the apartments, set them back from the building, and connected them by a bridge to the main structure. In this "summer room", as it is called to encourage sales, the residents sit between the tops of the surrounding plane trees, whose leaves provide shade, so that you can almost feel as though you are in a tree house. The architect had the trees measured three-dimensionally, in order not to have to fell any branches, and to situate the boxes precisely in the open spaces between them. Unfortunately, the trees were damaged in a storm, so that today, only the irregular arrangement of the boxes is a reminder of the branches that have vanished. In the meantime, the trees have recovered and the residents can once again sit in the middle of a green zone. Anyone who is not fortunate enough to live in an apartment with a "summer room" does not in the least have to make do with conventional living. To emphasize the feeling of sitting in the outdoors, the balconies of the remaining apartments extend unusually far outwards and instead of being enclosed by a normal balustrade, they are surrounded by a wooden garden fence.

Die Idee eines Baumhauses stand Pate, als der Architekt Eduard Francois für eine Wohnanlage in Montpellier eine neue Art von Balkon erfand: Er stellte eine begehbare Box ohne Dach vor die Wohnungen, rückte sie vom Gebäude ab und verband sie über einen Steg mit dem Bauwerk. In diesem „Sommerzimmer", wie es verkaufsfördernd genannt wurde, sitzen die Benutzer zwischen den Kronen der umgebenden Platanen, deren Blätter Schatten spenden, so dass man sich fast wie in einem Baumhaus fühlen kann. Um keine Äste absägen zu müssen, ließ der Architekt die Bäume dreidimensional vermessen und die Boxen exakt in die Freiräume dazwischen einpassen. Leider fiel das Grün einem Sturm zum Opfer und heute erinnert nur noch die unregelmäßig versetzte Anordnung der Boxen an die verschwundenen Äste. Nachdem sich die Pflanzen inzwischen erholt haben, können die Bewohner nun wieder mitten im Grünen sitzen. Wer nicht das Glück hat, eines der Apartments mit „Sommerzimmer" zu bewohnen, muss sich dennoch keineswegs mit Konventionellem begnügen, denn auch für die Freibereiche der übrigen Wohnungen hat sich der Architekt etwas einfallen lassen. Um das Gefühl, im Freien zu sitzen, zu unterstützen, kragen die Balkone ungewöhnlich weit aus und werden statt von einem normalen Geländer von einem hölzernen Gartenzaun eingefasst.

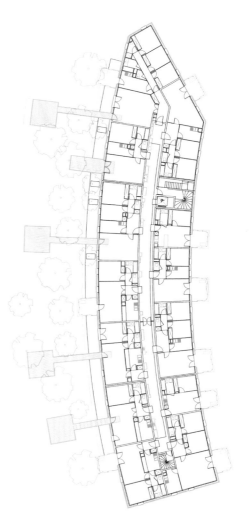

balkone nikolaistraße | munich . germany
DESIGN: Hild und K Architekten

What can be done when the rear courtyard balcony of a nine-teenth century building needs to be renovated and replaced, but the standard solution of a structure built onto the façade is out of the question, because parking spaces in the courtyard would be lost? And how is it possible to keep the reference to the old, ornamental iron fretwork railings by optics and surface feel? The architects decide to hang the new balconies like crates in front of the façade. The railings are made of corrugated steel with a floral motif, which is adopted from a stucco ornament on the street side. With the help of a computer, a photo of this original decoration was reduced in a grid scheme and cut out of the corrugated steel plates by laser cutting technology. The construction itself also required a certain degree of skill. By means of two central holes bored at the height of the railing through the façade and the walls behind, two, two meter long threaded posts were built in. They are anchored into the stonework by an injection gun and make it possible to hang the completely ready-made balcony. The surfaces of the balustrade, steel supports, floor plate and surrounding flower troughs made out of flat steel were welded together and form a self-carrying construction, statically, as a total system.

Was tun, wenn die Hinterhofbalkone eines Gründerzeithauses baufällig werden und ersetzt werden müssen, die Standardlösung mit einer vor die Fassade gestellten Konstruktion aber nicht in Frage kommt, weil dadurch Parkplätze im Hof verloren gehen würden? Und wie schafft man es, den ehemals ornamentalen schmiedeeisernen Geländern durch Optik und Haptik Referenz zu erweisen? Die Architekten entschieden sich, die neuen Balkone wie Kästen vor die Fassade zu hängen. Die Brüstungen bestehen aus Stahlblechen mit einem floralen Motiv, das einem Stuckornament der Straßenseite entnommen ist. Mit Hilfe des Computers wurde ein Foto dieser Ursprungsverzierung in Bandraster aufgelöst und durch ein Laserschneideverfahren aus den Stahlblechtafeln herausgeschnitten. Auch die Konstruktion erforderte ein gewisses Maß an Raffinesse. Mittels zwei Kernbohrungen auf Brüstungshöhe durch die Fassade und die dahinter liegenden Mauern wurden zwei Gewindestangen von zwei Meter Länge eingelassen. Sie sind durch einen Injektionskleber im Mauerwerk verankert und ermöglichen die Aufhängung des komplett vorgefertigten Balkons. Geländerflächen, Stahlträger, Bodenplatte und die umlaufenden Blumenkästen aus Flachstahl sind miteinander verschweißt und bilden eine selbsttragende Konstruktion als statisches Gesamtsystem.

wolkenstein | meran . italy

DESIGN: Holz Box Tirol + DI Anton Höss

Marquees and sunshades usually spell the death of every architecture with ambition. For that reason, the architects of a four-storey residential building in Meran have taken precautions: to prevent unregulated design elements appearing at random on the balconies of the twelve apartments, they equipped each outdoor space with a textile membrane, stretched over a vertical steel frame and protecting half of every balcony from onlookers and the sun's rays. The colored textiles in chess-board pattern are distributed over the different storeys, an arrangement that emerged from the mirroring of the apartment architectural design on each storey. As every fabric sail displays a different color, it gives each apartment an individual note, although the façade still looks as though it is designed uniformly. Ready-made, solid panels of treated pinewood serve for the construction of the balconies and the remaining building. They project as a wall section, carry the flooring in the outdoor areas and function as a partition wall. The upper layer of the balcony floors is made of glued pinewood, which is more weather-resistant.

Markisen und Sonnenschirme sind meist der Tod jeder ambitionierten Architektur. Deshalb sorgten die Architekten einer viergeschossigen Wohnanlage in Meran vor: Um gestalterischen Wildwuchs an den Balkonen der zwölf Wohnungen zu verhindern, statteten sie jeden Freisitz mit einer textilen Membran aus, die über einen vertikalen Stahlrahmen gespannt ist und die Hälfte jedes Balkons vor Einblicken und Sonnenstrahlen schützt. Im Schachbrettmuster verteilen sich die eingefärbten Stoffe über die Etagen, eine Anordnung, die sich aus den geschossweise gespiegelten Wohnungsgrundrissen ergibt. Da jedes Stoffsegel in einer anderen Farbe leuchtet, gibt es der Wohnung jeweils eine individuelle Note, dennoch wirkt die Fassade einheitlich gestaltet. Zur Konstruktion der Balkone wie auch des restlichen Gebäudes dienen vorgefertigte Massivtafeln aus verleimtem Tannenholz. Sie kragen als Wandscheibe aus, tragen die Bodenplatten der Freisitze und fungieren als Trennwand. Die oberste Schicht der Balkonböden besteht aus Lärchenholz, das witterungsbeständiger ist.

höttinger au | innsbruck . austria

DESIGN: Holz Box Tirol

An apartment building on the city limits of Innsbruck shows how a building can define the relationship of inside and outside in various different ways. On the north side, the interior space extends to the outside and window bays, glazed only above and at the sides, project outwards onto the street. Their front sides, in contrast, remain completely closed and are covered with a layer of oak, like the other external walls, blocking the view of the neighbouring building, while at the same time making it possible to look along the street and up to the mountains. The garden side in the south is defined by balconies made out of glass, whose front side can be opened or closed for the entire width, so that the outdoor seats are also utilized as a conservatory. Its front glazing, set in a steel construction, that extends right and left over the individual balconies and connects them with each other, can be pushed to one side, thus creating a constantly changing view. A balustrade of expanded metal prevents danger of falls. The characteristic extensions on the street and rear side of the building are to be regarded as a reference to the region's building history, they interpret traditional elements, such as the front window bay and the wooden bay of the garden façade, in a contemporary manner.

Wie ein Gebäude das Verhältnis von innen und außen auf sehr unterschiedliche Weise definieren kann, zeigt ein Mehrfamilienhaus am Stadtrand von Innsbruck. Auf seiner Nordseite stülpt sich der Innenraum nach außen und es dringen Erker in den Straßenraum vor, die nur oben und seitlich verglast sind. Ihre Vorderfronten dagegen, die wie die übrigen Außenwände eine Eichenholzverschalung tragen, bleiben komplett geschlossen und versperren den Blick auf die gegenüberliegende Bebauung, während sie gleichzeitig ermöglichen, die Straße entlang auf die Berge zu sehen. Der Gartenseite im Süden sind rundum verglaste Balkone vorgelagert, deren Vorderfront je nach Bedarf auf ganzer Breite zu öffnen oder schließen ist, so dass die Freisitze auch als Wintergärten nutzbar sind. Ihre Frontscheibe lässt sich in einer Stahlkonstruktion, die rechts und links über die einzelnen Balkone hinausragt und sie miteinander verbindet, zur Seite schieben, so dass eine ständig variierende Ansicht entsteht. Als Absturzsicherung dient ein Geländer aus Streckmetall. Die charakteristischen Auskragungen auf Straßen- und Rückseite des Gebäudes sind als eine Referenz an die regionale Baugeschichte zu verstehen, sie interpretieren traditionelle Elemente wie den Fronterker und den hölzernen Erker der Gartenfassaden auf zeitgenössische Weise.

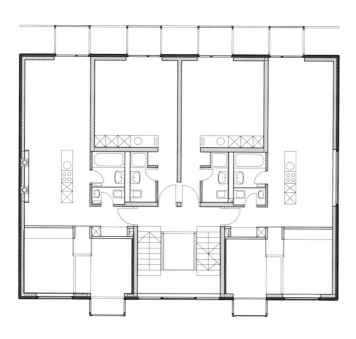

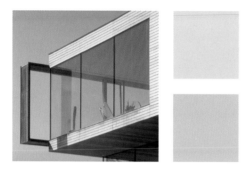

haus sauter | lindau . germany

DESIGN: k_m architektur DI Arch. Daniel Sauter

Wood is the predominant material of a villa near Lindau. It not only forms the external skin, but was introduced as a construction material, so that the detached house could be constructed thanks to an elementary building method in the record time of three months. A box of 20 by 11 meters seems to be suspended above a glazed, plinth level and a concrete bracket. It extends unusually far outwards, as though it is trying to reach towards the view, since the two loggias that are integrated into it provide an excellent view of the mountain landscape of the Vorarlberg region and Switzerland. Everything seems focused on this view. The direction of the parquet in the inside is taken up both in the cedar wooden floor of the loggia and the wooden cladding on the walls and ceiling and directs the view towards the outside and to the surroundings. A frameless window, which does not trap the view, underlines this effect. The view from the larger loggia is then rather restrained by a closed balustrade, but from the smaller loggia, which scarcely has a balustrade only of two horizontal cross-posts, the eye can sweep into the distance.

Holz ist das dominierende Material einer Villa bei Lindau. Es bildet nicht nur die Außenhaut, sondern wurde auch als Konstruktionsmaterial eingesetzt, so dass sich das Einfamilienhaus dank elementierter Bauweise in der Rekordzeit von drei Monaten errichten ließ. Eine Box von 20 mal 11 Metern scheint über einem verglasten Sockelgeschoss und einem Betonbügel zu schweben. Sie kragt ungewöhnlich weit aus, als wolle sie sich der Aussicht entgegenstrecken, denn von den beiden integrierten Loggien bietet sich eine ausgezeichnete Fernsicht auf die Berglandschaft von Vorarlberg und der Schweiz. Alles scheint auf diesen Ausblick fokussiert. Die Richtung des Parketts im Innenraum setzt sich sowohl in den Zedernholzdielen am Boden der Loggia als auch in der Bretterschalung an Wänden und Decke fort und lenkt den Blick nach draußen auf die Umgebung. Eine rahmenlose Verglasung, an der das Auge nicht hängen bleiben kann, unterstützt diesen Effekt. Während der Blick bei der größeren Loggia dann von einer geschlossenen Brüstung etwas gebremst wird, kann er bei der kleineren durch ein Nichts von Geländer, das nur aus zwei horizontalen Querstangen besteht, in die Ferne schweifen.

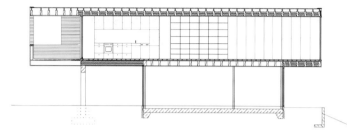

stadstuinen | rotterdam . netherlands

DESIGN: KCAP Architects & Planners

The Stadstuinen project shows how balconies and conservatories overcome monotony in a residential complex. The KCAP office planned a block perimeter of 16 four and eight storey apartment blocks for an area of 60,000 square meters. These can be clearly recognized as a unified structure, because the same, brightly colored clinker on each building joins them optically together. At the same time, however, building plans and elevation vary, because the density of the projecting balconies and conservatories changes, depending on each building's location, or on traffic conditions. A potential tenant could, in principle, form an opinion about traffic density just by looking at them. For instance, a façade located on a busy traffic route is so covered with glass window bays that they almost form a second skin, in order to keep the traffic noise from the apartments behind. They are scattered across the façade in a chequered pattern, while the upper side is also often used as a balcony. On another building, they carry the galleries situated above. As these outdoor areas—both the glazed and open ones—are furnished by residents in a quite individual way, they create a bright and differentiated picture on the façade.

Wie man mit Balkonen und Wintergärten Monotonie in einer Siedlung vermeidet, führt das Projekt Stadstuinen vor. Für ein Gebiet von 60.000 Quadratmetern in Rotterdam plante das Büro KCAP eine Blockrandbebauung mit 16 vier- bzw. achtgeschossigen Wohnhäusern. Diese lassen sich zwar deutlich als eine Einheit erkennen, denn dieselben bunt eingefärbten Klinker an allen Gebäuden fassen sie optisch zusammen; gleichzeitig variieren die Bauwerke jedoch in Grundriss und Ansicht, weil je nach Lage des Gebäudes oder den Verkehrsgegebenheiten die Dichte der vorgehängten Balkone und Wintergärten wechselt. Ein potenzieller Mieter könnte prinzipiell beim Anblick der Häuser im Umkehrschluss auf die Straßenbelastung schließen. So ist etwa eine Fassade an einer stark befahrenen Straße derart dicht mit Glas-Erkern überzogen, dass diese fast eine zweite Außenhaut bilden, um den Straßenlärm von den dahinter liegenden Wohnungen abzuhalten. Schachbrettartig verteilen sie sich über die Fassade, wobei ihre Oberseite häufig auch als Balkon genutzt wird. An einem anderen Gebäude tragen sie die darüber liegenden Laubengänge. Da diese Freibereiche – sowohl die verglasten als auch die offenen – von den Bewohnern jeweils individuell möbliert werden, zeichnen sie ein buntes, abwechslungsreiches Bild auf die Fassade.

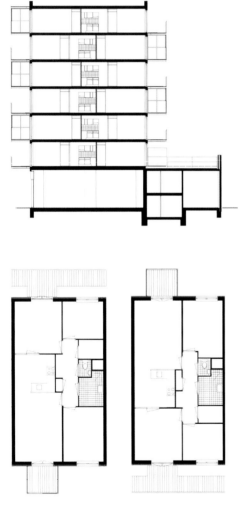

wozoko's | amsterdam . netherlands

DESIGN: MVRDV

In the Netherlands, a new policy for pensioners towards the end of the 1990s was to provide for "residential care complexes", which aimed to enable people above the age of 55 to continue living in their homes for as long as possible. An example of an old-age center with an option of minimal supervision was created in west Amsterdam. The problem of making the apartments individual, even though for cost reasons they have identical layouts and are stacked on top of each other, was brilliantly solved by the architects: the balconies situated on the south façade are in different sizes and proportions. Acrylic glass in a wide variety of colors serves as a balustrade element and provides each balcony with an individual identity. Different window sizes seem to be scattered at whim over the façade. They give a relaxed look and liven up the 100 meter long building, which is obviously also in demand with older people: when the building was opened, all the apartments were already taken.

Eine Trendwende in der Seniorenpolitik gegen Ende der neunziger Jahre sah in den Niederlanden „Wohnsorgekomplexe" mit dem Ziel vor, Personen ab 55 Jahren so lange wie möglich in den eigenen vier Wänden wohnen zu lassen. Im Westen Amsterdams ist ein solches Altenzentrum mit der Option auf geringe Betreuung entstanden. Das Problem, den Wohnungen, die aus Kostengründen mit immer gleichem Zuschnitt übereinander gestapelt werden müssen, dennoch Individualität zu verleihen, lösten die Architekten mit Bravour: Der Südfassade sind Balkone unterschiedlicher Größe und Proportion vorgelagert. Acrylglas in den verschiedensten Farben dient als Brüstungselement und gibt so jedem Vorbau seine eigene Identität. Unterschiedliche Fensterformate scheinen wahllos über die Außenhaut gestreut. Sie lockern die Ansicht auf und verleihen dem 100 Meter langen Gebäude eine Lebendigkeit, wie sie offensichtlich auch im fortgeschrittenen Alter gefragt ist: Bei Eröffnung des Bauwerks waren bereits alle Wohnungen vergeben.

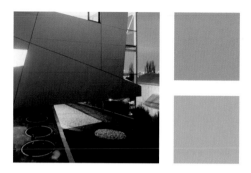

DRA einfamilienhaus | vienna . austria

DESIGN: querkraft

The house seems to fly. The Querkraft studio constructed a three-storey villa above a hill with a 25 degree incline on the city limits of Vienna. The building extends up to two thirds over the slope and creates a sheltered open-air space. This is made possible by a two-storey construction of a steel space frame, which is anchored on the concrete lower storey and permits free floorplan layouts. The steel structure is encased in a skin of irregular, specially cut, polygonal aluminium sheets, whose splice-image does not suggest any conclusions about the design of the different levels or purpose of the rooms. Interventions in the casing serve as windows for the residents, or they expose a view of the skeleton, for instance, on the south-facing balconies, which give a fabulous view over Vienna. The loggias are integrated into the building by the surrounding façade's casing and they are not built onto the structure, as is so often the case. While the outdoor area is therefore clearly separated from the external space, the transition from the balcony area to the internal part of the building is almost invisible, thanks to room-high windows. The loggia floors made of trellis grids let a lot of light in and do not deprive the living areas of their lightness.

Das Haus scheint zu fliegen. Über einer Böschung mit 25 Grad Gefälle am Stadtrand von Wien errichtete das Büro Querkraft eine dreigeschossige Villa, die zu zwei Dritteln über den Abgrund ragt und damit eine überdachte Freifläche schafft. Möglich wird dies durch eine zweistöckige Konstruktion aus Fachwerkträgern, die auf dem betonierten Untergeschoss verankert ist und eine freie Raumaufteilung gestattet. Eingehüllt ist der Stahlbau in eine Haut aus unregelmäßig zugeschnittenen, polygonalen Aluminiumplatten, deren Fugenbild keine Rückschlüsse auf Geschossgliederung oder Raumfunktion zulässt. Einschnitte in die Hülle dienen den Bewohnern als Fenster oder geben den Blick auf das Skelett frei, etwa bei den südlich gelegenen Balkonen, von denen man eine traumhafte Aussicht auf Wien genießen kann. Durch die umlaufende Fassadenhaut sind die Loggien ins Gebäude integriert und nicht wie so oft üblich dem Bauwerk vorgelagert. Während der Freisitz vom Außenraum also deutlich getrennt ist, erfolgt der Übergang von der Balkonfläche ins Hausinnere dank raumhoher Fenster fast nahtlos. Die Loggiaböden aus Gitterrosten lassen viel Licht passieren und rauben den Wohnräumen nicht die Helligkeit.

living room | gelnhausen . germany

DESIGN: seifert.stoeckmann@formalhaut

In a small community near Frankfurt, one building attracts attention, since its abstract façade does not seem to want to integrate into the peaceful neighborhood—at first sight. At a closer look, the viewer observes that both in terms of size and contours, the building fits perfectly into the surroundings. The architects adopted the dimensions and geometry of the building's old predecessor and responded to the neighbouring half-timbered buildings with the chess-board style, closed and glazed façade arrangement, even if it was achieved in unfamiliar form. Anyone who is surprised at the idiosyncratic, external skin of the building might definitely be amazed by the fact that the gable side suddenly opens and a balcony projects outwards like a drawer. Powered by an electric motor, a part of the building's interior room moves towards the outside and towers over the heads of passers-by onto the street. This mobile room can be extended outwards up to 2.75 meters. In the interior of the building, which is formed as a large, open room as far as the roof, the extended space appears as a suspended box.

In einer kleinen Gemeinde in der Nähe Frankfurts erregt ein Gebäude Aufmerksamkeit, das sich mit seiner abstrakten Fassade so gar nicht in die beschauliche Umgebung einfügen möchte – auf den ersten Blick. Denn bei genauerem Hinsehen stellt der Betrachter fest, dass es sich in Größe und Umrisslinie perfekt der Umgebung anpasst. Die Architekten übernahmen Volumen und Geometrie des alten Vorgängerbaus und gingen mit den schachbrettartig angeordneten geschlossenen und verglasten Fassadenfeldern auf die Gliederung der benachbarten Fachwerkhäuser ein, wenn auch in verfremdeter Form. Wer sich schon über die eigenwillige Außenhaut des Bauwerks wundert, dürfte allerdings erst recht ins Staunen geraten, wenn sich plötzlich die Giebelseite öffnet und ein Balkon wie eine Schublade herausfährt. Von einem Elektromotor angetrieben schiebt sich ein Teil des Innenraums aus dem Bauwerk nach außen und ragt über die Köpfe der Passanten auf die Straße hinaus. Bis zu 2,75 Meter lässt sich dieser mobile Raum ausfahren. Im Gebäudeinneren, das als ein großer, bis unter das Dach offener Raum ausgebildet ist, tritt er als eingehängte Box in Erscheinung.

wohnDNA | gratkom . austria

DESIGN: DI Reinhold Weichlbauer, DI Albert Josef Ortis

An apartment building near Graz shows two faces. For the plot is located in a transitional zone between high-rise apartment blocks and detached housing. The architects use balconies and terraces, to integrate their building according to urban-planning categories: on one side, it emerges as a scarcely structured, large-scale form, while on the other side it reacts to its small-scale counterpart through the plastic formulation of open-air zones. Here, the balconies project outwards in an adventurous fashion. They seem to shoot out of the building like spikes and penetrate the exterior space. The terraces on the ground level are treated exactly as the balconies in terms of their design; they are bordered by the same boundary walls and therefore also form part of the overall sculpture, which the apartment building forms. This impression is also supported by the inclusion of the same, bright yellow color on all building elements and the same window format on all sides of the building. In some cases it is hard to distinguish at first sight whether a part of the building belongs to an indoor or outdoor space, since the windows not only penetrate the walls of the enclosed rooms, but also the balustrades of the balconies. The viewer occasionally looks into a kitchen or stairwell and occasionally simply at the blue sky.

Zwei Gesichter hat ein eigenwilliges Mehrfamilienhaus in der Nähe von Graz. Denn das Grundstück liegt in einem Übergangsbereich zwischen Geschosswohnblöcken und einem Einfamilienhausgebiet. Die Architekten nutzen Balkone und Terrassen, um ihr Gebäude städtebaulich einzupassen: Während es auf einer Seite als kaum gegliederte Großform auftritt, reagiert es auf der anderen Seite durch die plastische Ausformulierung der Freibereiche auf sein kleinteiliges Gegenüber. Hier ragen Balkone abenteuerlich weit aus und überdachen Hauszugänge, Terrassentüren oder Stellplätze. Wie Stacheln scheinen sie aus dem Bauwerk zu schießen und in den Außenraum vorzudringen. Die Terrassen im Erdgeschoss sind gestalterisch genau wie die Balkone behandelt; sie werden von den gleichen Umfassungsmauern begrenzt und sind daher auch Teil der Gesamtskulptur, die das Wohnhaus bildet – ein Eindruck, der auch durch den Einsatz des gleichen knallgelben Anstrichs auf allen Bauteilen und des gleichen Fensterformats auf allen Seiten des Gebäudes unterstützt wird. Wo bei dem Bau innen und außen liegen, ist auf den ersten Blick teils schwer auszumachen, denn die Fenster durchstoßen nicht nur die Wände der geschlossenen Räume, sondern auch die Balkonbrüstungen. Mal schaut der Betrachter in eine Küche oder ein Treppenhaus, mal aber auch einfach in den blauen Himmel.

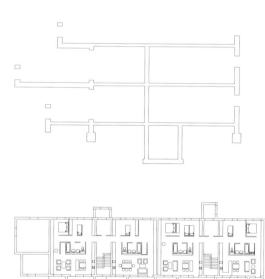

rooftops

haus ebeling | dortmund . germany
DESIGN: ArchiFactory.de

No roof extensions, rain gutters or canopies interrupt the monolithic appearance of the building, which was erected as an extension to a detached house. Mitred wooden planks and flush windows give the block an homogeneous appearance. The surprise: the cube is not as solid as it seems, in the upper storey, it houses a roof terrace, which cannot be seen from the outside. In contrast to the building's generous window openings, it appears like a hidden refuge. Walls as high as a single storey surround the area shielding from curious looks in the vicinity and making this an introverted outdoor area, which guarantees unrestricted private space and a feeling of absolute peace. The user can be near to the sky up here—in the truest sense of the word. Anyone who nevertheless feels like finding a better view can open narrow, collapsible elements, which give a view of the surroundings and when closed are hardly visible. As with the façade, the architects had the outer walls as well as the floor of the terrace constructed out of unplaned, untreated larchwood. This makes the minimalist impression more intense.

Keine Dachüberstände, Regenrinnen oder Vordächer stören die monolithische Wirkung des Baukörpers, der als Anbau an ein Einfamilienhaus errichtet wurde. Auf Gehrung geschnittene Holzplanken und außen bündig sitzende Fenster verleihen dem Block eine homogene Erscheinung. Die Überraschung: Der Kubus ist weniger massiv, als er erscheint, im oberen Geschoss beherbergt er eine Dachterrasse, die von außen nicht zu erkennen ist. Im Gegensatz zu den großflächigen Fensteröffnungen des Gebäudes präsentiert sie sich wie eine verschlossene Zuflucht. Geschosshohe Wände umgeben den Bereich, schützen vor neugierigen Blicken aus der Nachbarschaft und machen ihn zu einem introvertierten Außenraum, der eine uneingeschränkte Intimsphäre gewährt und ein Gefühl absoluter Ruhe vermittelt. Hier kann der Benutzer dem Himmel nah sein – im wahrsten Sinne des Wortes. Wem der Sinn dennoch einmal nach etwas mehr Aussicht steht, kann schmale Klappelemente öffnen, die einen Blick in die Umgebung ermöglichen, im geschlossenen Zustand aber kaum sichtbar sind. Wie die Fassade ließen die Architekten sowohl die Umfassungswände als auch den Terrassenboden aus sägerauen, unbehandelten Lärchenholzbohlen anfertigen. Dies intensiviert den minimalistischen Eindruck.

Eingangsebene

Wohnebene

Galerieebene

Patioebene

01 Foyer
02 Gäste-WC
03 Kellerräume
04 Garage
05 Wohnen
06 Küche / Essen
07 Terrasse
08 Galerie
09 Luftraum
10 Flur
11 Schlafen
12 Bad
13 Patio

Längsschnitt

haus ray1 | vienna . austria
DESIGN: Delugan Meissl Associated Architects

It almost appears as though a UFO has landed on the flat roof of the six-storey office block—or else it is just about to take off. The sculptural roof of a villa in Vienna's fourth district presents this process as though it had been frozen in an action shot. A long, extending beam, which is bent in several places provides both a sightscreen and guard rail on the terrace. The beam runs like a ribbon through the room and gives the building the dynamics, which have been mentioned. However, this construction is not just an aesthetic creation for its own ends, rather a steel skeleton is concealed behind the Alucobond cladding, which helps to divert the load of the construction to the fire partition walls. The external skin also defines the framework for the built-in furniture and enables the inventory to merge with the architecture in this way. Glass elements, which are the height of the room, closed surfaces, interventions and overlappings, as well as projections and recesses define the transparent and shielded areas on both sides of the narrow building. The penthouse is surrounded by three terraces, with one of them being defined by a pool at the level of the wooden floor, so that the view is not interrupted by railings and the city can be surveyed.

Fast scheint es, als sei ein UFO auf dem Flachdach des sechsgeschossigen Bürogebäudes gelandet – oder im Begriff gerade abzuheben. Als wäre dieser Prozess in einer Momentaufnahme eingefroren, präsentiert sich die skulpturale Dachvilla im vierten Wiener Bezirk. Ein lang gestreckter, mehrfach geknickter Balken, der zugleich Sichtschutz und Absturzsicherung für die Terrasse ist, zieht sich wie eine Schleife durch den Raum und verleiht dem Gebäude die angesprochene Dynamik. Doch diese Konstruktion ist kein ästhetischer Selbstzweck, vielmehr verbirgt sich hinter der Alucobondverkleidung ein Stahlskelett, mit dessen Hilfe die Lasten des Aufbaus über die seitlichen Brandmauern abgeleitet werden. Zugleich gibt die Außenhaut den Rahmen der Einbaumöbel vor und lässt auf diese Weise die Architektur mit dem Inventar verschmelzen. Raumhohe Glaselemente, geschlossene Flächen, Einschnitte und Überlagerungen sowie Vor- und Rücksprünge definieren auf beiden Seiten des schmalen Gebäudes transparente und geschützte Zonen. Drei Terrassen umgeben das Penthouse, von denen eine durch ein dem Holzboden höhengleiches Wasserbecken begrenzt wird, so dass der Blick ohne von einer Brüstung gestört zu werden über die Stadt schweifen kann.

wohngebäude paltramplatz | vienna . austria

DESIGN: Delugan Meissl Associated Architects

In one of the most densely populated district's of Vienna, the Favoriten district, at one of the precinct's squares, the passer-by is confronted with the sharp edges of a cube which is covered with black concrete fiber sheets. Windows and loggia boxes, which have been playfully distributed, lighten up the façade and allow the building to appear like a bureau with drawers opened up to various extents. A distinctive polygonal, steel roof is visible if you look upwards. It has been punched with holes to allow the light through. Through these openings, sun and full moon create a pattern of light points on the façade. The perforated roof construction is designed to characterize the upper part of the building in a striking way, since a special facility is located there: a large terrace, a sauna and rest room that are open to all residents as a relaxing oasis in the city. Photovoltaic cells contribute to the ecologic electricity supply of the common rooms. The roof was horizontally rotated against the rest of the building and extends far outwards. What the passer-by cannot recognize from below: the roof also covers the terraces of the apartments on the attic level, that are recessed from the façade. For the three apartments, this area provides a hidden sanctuary.

In Favoriten, dem bevölkerungsreichsten Stadtteil Wiens, der trotz wirtschaftlicher Veränderung immer noch als Arbeiter- und Industriebezirk gilt, begegnet dem Passanten an einem Quartiersplatz ein scharfkantiger, mit schwarzen Zementfaserplatten verkleideter Kubus. Spielerisch verteilte Fenster und Loggia-Boxen lockern die Fassade auf und lassen die Eckbebauung wie eine Kommode mit unterschiedlich geöffneten Schubladen wirken. Beim Blick nach oben wird eine markante, polygonale Überdachung aus Stahlblech sichtbar, das aus Belichtungsgründen gelocht wurde. Sonne und Vollmond zeichnen durch diese Öffnungen ein Muster aus Lichtpunkten auf die Fassade. Die perforierte Dachkonstruktion will den oberen Abschluss des Hauses auffallend kennzeichnen, denn dort befindet sich ein besonderer Ort: Ein großer, allgemein zugänglicher Terrassenbereich mit Sauna- und Ruheraum dient allen Hausbewohnern als erholsame Stadt-Oase. Photovoltaikzellen tragen zur umweltfreundlichen Stromversorgung der Gemeinschaftsräume bei. Das Dach wurde horizontal gegen den Rest des Bauwerks verdreht und kragt weit in den Straßenraum aus. Was der Passant von unten nicht erahnt: Es überdeckt auch die Balkone, die den Wohnungen im oberen Stockwerk vorgelagert sind, das als Attikageschoss von der Fassade zurückspringt. Für drei Wohneinheiten bietet sich hier ein verstecktes Refugium.

reihenhäuser sistrans | sistrans . austria

DESIGN: Holz Box Tirol

How can lots of living space be created with not much money? This question is answered by a terraced housing site in the Tirole. In addition to the compact building typology, a high level of ready-made elements also helped to reduce the costs. The entrance level was the only floor to be built on location, all other storeys above this were supplied as ready made parts: as with a building block system, ceilings, walls, complete bathrooms and kitchens were stacked, fixed and screwed together on site. The houses now stand in a terrace, in an integrated rhythm and a south-facing location and they have their own south-facing garden; the large terrace on the ground floor and the balcony on the upper storey are located on the eastern side. The best spot for sun-bathing and a panoramic view over the Tirolian landscape is offered by the roof-top terrace. The terrace was given an extremely filigree railing, so as not to disrupt the rhythm of the wooden boxes and the cube of the building. A net, which is stretched over a steel frame, is hardly visible from a distance and almost dissolves the balustrade into obscurity. On the one hand, what gives the residents unlimited views, such as when they relax on sun-loungers on the roof terrace is in contrast nothing for people with vertigo.

Wie lässt sich viel Wohnraum mit wenig Geld schaffen? Diese Frage beantwortet eine Reihenhausanlage in Tirol. Neben der kompakten Bauweise half vor allem der hohe Vorfertigungsgrad, die Kosten zu senken. Denn lediglich das Eingangsgeschoss wurde vor Ort in den Hang hineinbetoniert, alle darüber liegenden Stockwerke als Fertigteile angeliefert. Wie bei einem Baukastensystem wurden vor Ort Decken, Wände, komplette Badezimmer und Küchen gestapelt, gesteckt und verschraubt. In gleichmäßigem Rhythmus reihen sich die Häuser nun aneinander, sie sind nach Süden ausgerichtet und verfügen über einen eigenen Garten in Südlage; die große Terrasse im Erdgeschoss und der Balkon im Obergeschoss liegen auf der Ostseite. Die beste Besonnung und einen Panoramablick über die Tiroler Landschaft bietet jedoch die Terrasse auf dem Dachgeschoss. Um den Rhythmus der Holzboxen und die Gebäudekubatur nicht zu stören, erhielt die Terrasse ein extrem filigranes Geländer. Ein Netz, das sich über einen Stahlrahmen spannt, ist aus der Ferne kaum zu erkennen und löst das Geländer fast ins Unsichtbare auf. Was den Bewohnern einerseits uneingeschränkte Aussicht gewährt, etwa wenn sie im Liegestuhl auf der Dachterrasse entspannen, ist andererseits nichts für Menschen mit Höhenangst.

breevaarthoek | gouda . netherlands

DESIGN: KCAP Architects & Planners

A residential estate with differentiated outdoor areas was created in Gouda, in the Netherlands. The former industrial site is bordered in the west and south by two heavy traffic routes, to the east it opens onto the leisure zone of the Reeywiik lakes. So it is obvious that the architects oriented the buildings towards the best side. The most striking feature of the design are two tall brick buildings, which are located in the south of the site. Their individual floors are displaced against each other in a diagonal, almost step-like fashion, so that an outdoor area is formed for every unit, from which the residents can enjoy the view of the lake. The idea is continued for the two, flatter rows of terraced houses. They also look like cubes, which have been stacked onto each other and recessed to provide roof terraces on the upper floors. Due to lesser heights the railings could be constructed in a visibly narrower manner. This is why glass panels were used, which do not obscure the view. To preserve the relaxing view of the landscape for all residents of the development, the terraced houses towards the lake were perforated at irregular intervals. At least from their upper floors, residents in the second row can this way look over the gardens and watch the boats sailing between water lilies.

Eine Siedlung mit differenziertem Freiraumangebot entstand im holländischen Gouda. Die ehemalige Industriebrache wird im Westen und Süden von zwei stark befahrenen Durchgangsstraßen begrenzt, zum Osten öffnet sie sich dem Erholungsgebiet der Reeuwijk-Seen. So leuchtet es ein, dass die Architekten ihren Entwurf zur Schokoladenseite ausrichten. Markantester Punkt der Anlage sind zwei im Süden gelegene höhere backsteinverkleidete Baukörper. Ihre einzelnen Geschosse sind in der Diagonalen treppenartig gegeneinander verschoben, so dass sich für jede Einheit ein Freibereich bildet, von dem die Bewohner den Blick auf den See genießen können. Bei den zwei flacheren Reihenhauszeilen setzt sich das Konzept fort. Auch sie wirken wie übereinandergestapelte Kuben, die durch Rücksprünge im Obergeschoss Dachterrassen freigeben. Das Geländer konnte hier, wo die Absturzhöhe niedriger ist, deutlich schlanker ausfallen, so dass eine Glasscheibe zum Einsatz kam, welche die Aussicht nicht behindert. Um allen Bewohnern der Anlage den erholsamen Blick aufs Wasser zu ermöglichen, wurde die Zeile der am See gelegenen Reihenhäuser unregelmäßig perforiert. Auf diese Weise können auch die Bewohner aus der zweiten Reihe – zumindest vom obersten Geschoss aus – über die Gartenanlage hinweg auf vorbeifahrende Boote zwischen Seerosen blicken.

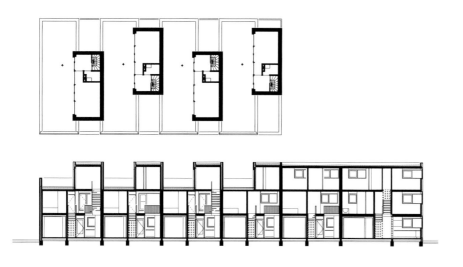

lukas-areal | dresden . germany

DESIGN: Müller Reimann Architekten

The Lukas-Areal in Dresden makes it possible to live near the city center in peaceful, almost suburban surroundings, yet the residential site is only within 10 minutes walking distance from the center. 39 terraced houses are concealed behind a five-storey building located near the university and railway station. A differentiated range of outdoor spaces is available for residents: from the ground floor, you enter a small garden, which is located 1.2 meters above street level to shield residents a little from curious looks of passers-by. Sunbathes can be taken on the top level of the three storeys. Terraces located here provide a degree of protected privacy that is unusual for terraced houses; since they are surrounded by walls on four sides, they almost look like an interior room. To the south, they feature openings covered by a lintel that look like windows. Movable red lacquered wooden blinds almost introduce a holiday feeling reminiscent of a Mediterranean resort. In the tradition of classical Modernism, all buildings were designed uniformly, the individual house is subordinate to the whole.

Innenstadtnahes Wohnen ermöglicht das Lukas-Areal in Dresden. Nur zehn Gehminuten vom Zentrum entfernt lässt es sich hier so ruhig leben wie in einer Vorstadtsiedlung. 39 Reihenhäuser verbergen sich hinter einer fünfgeschossigen Bebauung in der Nähe von Universität und Bahnhof. Ein differenziertes Freiraumangebot steht den Bewohnern zur Verfügung: Vom Erdgeschoss aus betritt man je einen kleinen Garten, der 1,2 Meter über dem Straßenniveau liegt, so dass man vor neugierigen Blicken der Passanten ein wenig geschützt ist. Im obersten der drei Geschosse lässt sich auf der Dachterrasse ein Sonnenbad nehmen. Sie bietet ein Maß an abgeschirmter Privatheit, das für Reihenhäuser ungewöhnlich ist. Da die Terrasse auf vier Seiten von Mauern eingefasst wird, wirkt sie fast wie ein Innenraum, die Öffnung nach Süden, von einem Sturz überspannt, erscheint als Fenster. Rot lackierte Lamellenschiebeläden aus Holz lassen beinahe die Urlaubsstimmung einer mediterranen Feriensiedlung aufkommen. In der Tradition der klassischen Moderne wurden alle Gebäude einheitlich gestaltet, das einzelne Haus ordnet sich dem Ganzen unter.

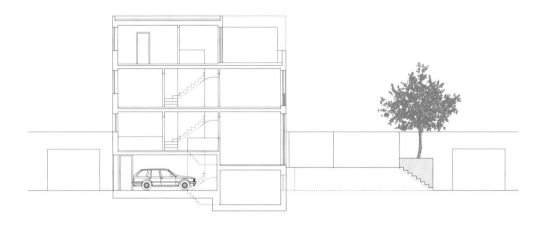

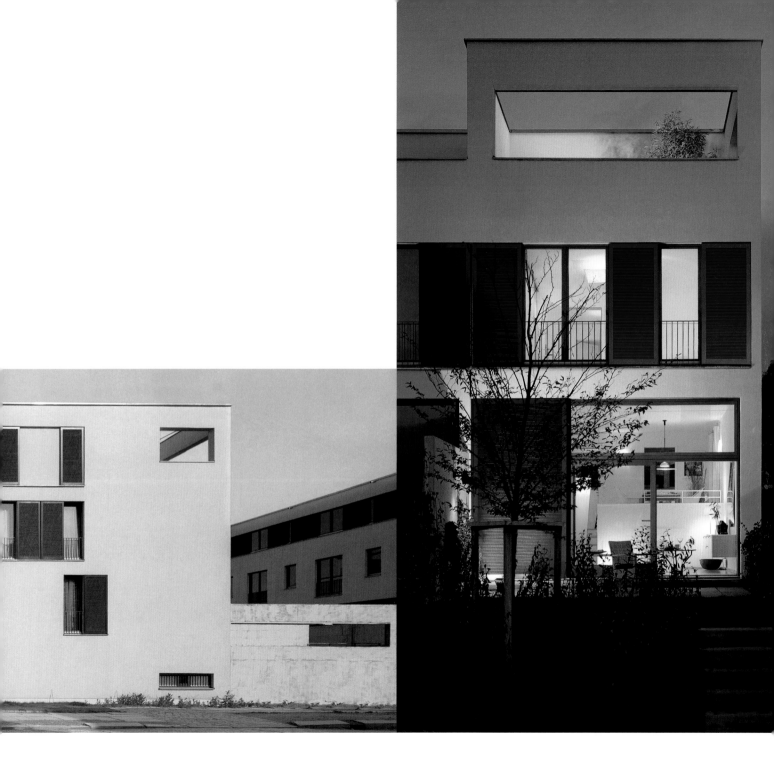

reihenhäuser küsnacht | küsnacht . switzerland

DESIGN: Barbara Weber & Bruno Oertli

Plots located around Lake Zurich are in high demand, especially when they offer a lake view and a sunny, sloping spot. Three terraced houses, which conform to the luxury of the surroundings, were built in a district of detached houses in the community of Küsnacht. A split-level organization makes it possible to experience the slope inside the house as well as to embed three storeys into the hillside without disturbing the neighbors' view. The site was maximally used, so that little space remained for garden areas. The terrace courtyard in the east and the west-facing double-height balcony counterbalance this deficit. They are bathed in sunshine almost the entire day. The house is crowned—in a literal sense—by a roof terrace with a lake view. A construction of slim steel struts frames the open, summer-like living room, the larch-wood floor and a sun-sail attached to the steel frame give a Mediterranean atmosphere. Filigree steel trellises, which were used as a railing for the roof terraces and balconies, correct the heaviness in the compact terraced houses.

Grundstücke rund um den Zürichsee sind sehr gefragt, insbesondere wenn sie mit Seeblick und sonniger Hanglage aufwarten. In einem Einfamilienhausquartier der Gemeinde Küsnacht entstanden drei Reihenhäuser, die dem Luxus der Umgebung entsprechen. Eingebettet in die Böschung ermöglicht eine Split-Level-Organisation, die den Hang auch im Inneren des Gebäudes erlebbar macht, drei Ebenen, ohne die Aussicht der Nachbarn zu stören. Da das Grundstück optimal ausgenutzt wurde, blieb nur wenig Platz für Gartenflächen. Als Ausgleich dienen der im Osten gelegene Terrassenhof hinter dem Haus sowie der nach Westen orientierte Balkon über zwei Geschosse, die fast den ganzen Tag über Sonne bieten. Gekrönt – im buchstäblichen Sinne – wird das Haus durch eine Dachterrasse mit Aussicht auf den See. Eine Konstruktion aus schlanken Stahlprofilen rahmt den offenen, sommerlichen Wohnraum ein, der Boden aus Lärchenholzbohlen und ein zwischen das Stahlgerüst gespanntes Sonnensegel verleihen ihm eine mediterrane Atmosphäre. Filigrane Stahlgitter, die als Geländer für Dachterrasse und Balkone verwendet wurden, nehmen den kompakten Reihenhäusern die Schwere.

QUERSCHNITT

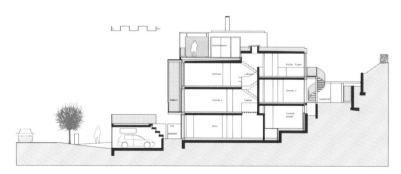

courtyards

haus göppner | ramstein . germany

DESIGN: bayer uhrig Architekten BDA

At the 2004 Venice Biennale, a detached house from Ramstein was shown among others. Perhaps it was nominated as a German entry because it is located in a typical German commuter neighborhood and makes the best of bad conditions there. It lacks a traditional garden, because in view of the density of neighboring houses, this would in any case provide little quality. Instead, the building extends as far as possible to the outer boundaries of the plot. To compensate, it provides a courtyard, which is enclosed on three sides by the building and therefore can only be overlooked from one side. The courtyard separates the bedroom from the living space. The transition from outside to inside is emphasized by oversized plaster-work frames around windows and doors. These frames are distinguished by color from the rest of the façade and are displaced on all sides in relation to the window. Although the idiosyncratic building with its patio creates a contrast to the neighborhood, nevertheless, it does not form a foreign body within its environs. Its scale—a single spread-out storey, covered by a flat gabled roof—fulfills the ususal conventions for this location, only to undermine them again with the courtyard.

Auf der Biennale in Venedig wurde im Jahr 2004 unter anderem ein Einfamilienhaus aus Ramstein präsentiert. Vielleicht wurde es für den deutschen Beitrag ausgewählt, weil es in einer typisch deutschen Vorstadt steht und aus den dortigen Missständen das Beste macht. Es verzichtet auf einen gewöhnlichen Garten, weil dieser angesichts der dichten Nachbarbebauung ohnehin wenig Aufenthaltsqualität bieten würde, und rückt stattdessen so nahe wie möglich an die Grundstücksgrenzen. Zum Ausgleich hält es aber einen Hof bereit, der auf drei Seiten vom Gebäude umschlossen wird, also nur von einer Seite einsehbar ist. Er trennt den Schlaf- vom Wohnbereich. Den Übergang von außen nach innen akzentuieren überbreite Putzrahmen an Fenstern und Türen, die farblich vom Rest der Fassade abgesetzt und gegen die Öffnungen, die sie einfassen, verschoben sind. Obwohl die eigenwillige Behausung sich mit ihrem Patio von der Umgebung abwendet, bildet sie dennoch keinen Fremdkörper im Quartier. Durch ihr Volumen – eingeschossig, breit gelagert und mit flach geneigtem Satteldach – erfüllt sie die ortsüblichen Konventionen, um sie gleichzeitig mit dem Hof wieder zu unterwandern.

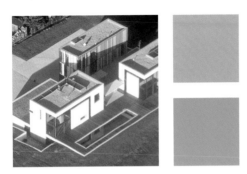

SML | burgrieden . germany

DESIGN: Titus Bernhard Architekten

On an agricultural site on the city limits of Burgrieden, between the residential site and open fields, an ensemble of three buildings is located, which together surround a courtyard. The builders are Suzanne, Marc and Lars Weidt, hence the name, SML. The two brothers, one a designer and the other an insurance salesman, each live in one building with their family and the design studio is located in the third building. A concrete plinth of 40 by 27 meters, which incorporates the cellar and garage, is located on the slighlty north-sloping hill and forms a plateau, on which the three buildings are situated. The plateau integrates the three structures like a frame, lifts them onto the pedestal, distinguishes them from the vicinity and makes it possible to unravel a sculptural effect. The remaining space between the two solid and the glass structure is filled with a courtyard of a special quality: on the one hand, it is clearly framed and protected by the buildings, on the other hand, it does not enclose, because it guarantees views between and past the three buildings. The restriction to a few materials—white plaster, colorful printed glass on the walls, gravel on the floor, concrete for the bench and open-air shower—gives the location it's tranquillity.

Auf einem landwirtschaftlichen Grundstück am Ortsrand von Burgrieden, am Übergang von Siedlung und freiem Feld, steht ein Ensemble von drei Gebäuden, die gemeinsam einen Hof umschließen. Bauherren sind Suzanne, Marc und Lars Weidt, daher der Name SML. Die beiden Brüder, ein Designer und ein Versicherungskaufmann, bewohnen mit Familie je ein Gebäude, im dritten ist das Designbüro untergebracht. Ein Betonsockel von 40 mal 27 Metern, der Keller und Garage aufnimmt, schiebt sich in den sanft nach Norden abfallenden Hang und bildet ein Plateau, auf das die drei Bauten gestellt sind. Wie ein Rahmen fasst das Plateau die drei Körper zusammen, hebt sie aufs Podest, separiert sie von der Umgebung und ermöglicht ihnen, ihre skulpturale Wirkung zu entfalten. Der verbleibende Raum zwischen den beiden massiven und dem verglasten Körper ergibt einen Hof von besonderer Qualität: Einerseits wird er von den Gebäuden deutlich gefasst und geschützt, andererseits engt er nicht ein, weil er Ausblicke zwischen den drei Bauten hindurch gewährt. Die Beschränkung auf wenige Materialien – weißer Putz und farbig bedrucktes Glas an den Wänden, Kies am Boden, Beton bei Bank und Freiluftdusche – verleiht ihm Ruhe.

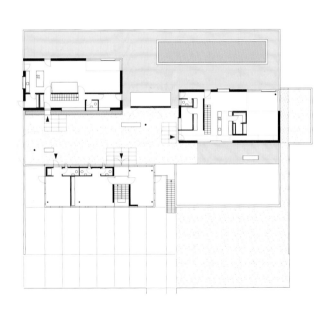

paul-lincke-höfe | berlin . germany

DESIGN: Langhof GmbH + Martha Schwartz

At the Paul-Lincke-bank in the middle of Berlin, in Kreuzberg, a factory building was renovated, extended and a new structure was added. 116 loft units were created, which group themselves around five courtyards. The landscape architect, Martha Schwartz created five "Paradise Gardens", which each have a key theme from one of Grimm's fairytales. She therefore adopts a tradition of garden design, where "fascinating locations" with fairytale surroundings make it possible to forget everyday life and are meant to offer people possibilities of retreating into another reality. However, she does not display the entire tale in the courtyard sites, but merely a picture that reflects the fairytale atmosphere. Residents are to be put in a positive mood by playful, colorful elements. Modern form language, combined with traces and structures from the past, lend the location a special power of attraction.

Mitten in Berlin, am Paul-Lincke-Ufer in Kreuzberg, wurde ein Fabrikgebäude umgebaut, aufgestockt und durch einen Neubau ergänzt. Entstanden sind 116 Loft-Einheiten, die sich um fünf Hofgärten gruppieren. Die Landschaftsarchitektin Martha Schwartz schuf fünf „Paradiesische Gärten", die je ein Leitmotiv eines Grimm'schen Märchens zeigen. Sie greift damit eine Tradition der Gartengestaltung auf, bei der „faszinierende Orte" mit märchenhaften Umgebungen den Alltag vergessen lassen und den Menschen Rückzugsmöglichkeiten in eine andere Wirklichkeit bieten sollen. Bei den Hofanlagen stellt sie jedoch nicht die gesamte Erzählung dar, sondern lediglich ein Bild, das die Atmosphäre des Märchens widerspiegelt. Die Bewohner sollen durch verspielte, farbenfrohe Elemente in eine positive Stimmung versetzt werden. Moderne Formensprache kombiniert mit Spuren und Strukturen aus der Vergangenheit verleihen dem Ort eine besondere Anziehungskraft.

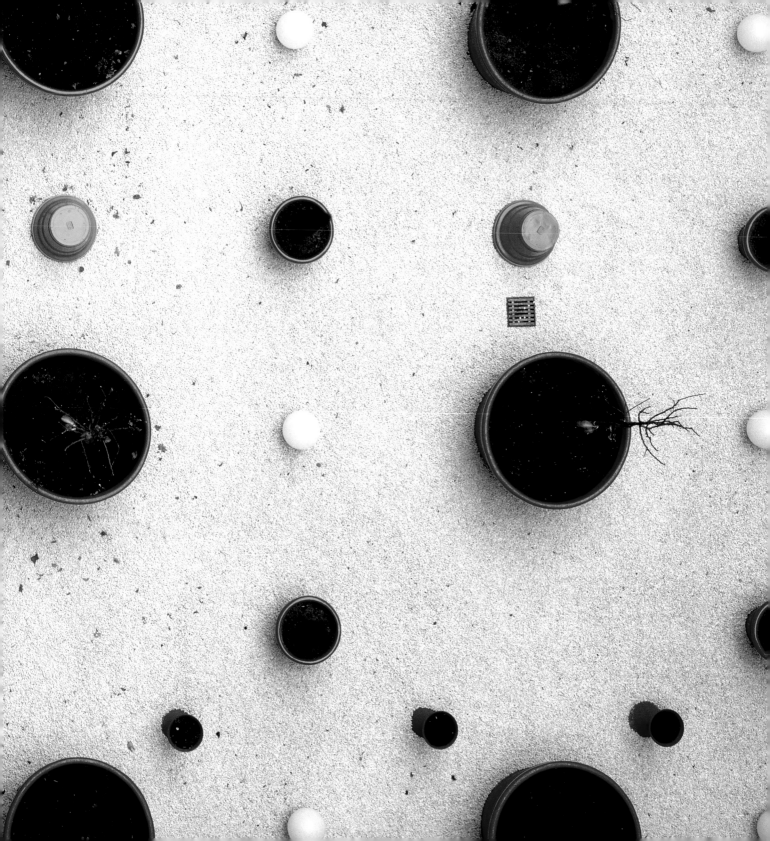

haus im münsterland | münsterland . germany
DESIGN: Léon Wohlhage Wernik Architekten

A house in Münsterland serves as a sanctuary, a quiet refuge for its owners to work and live in. The architects designed the building in a suitably quiet and reserved fashion; the rough materials and the rigid minimalism are unusual for a detached house. Steel frames cut razor-sharp openings in the raw concrete of the façade whose naked wall surfaces serve as a projection screen for the play of shadows from the trees. In front of the building, courtyards surrounded by storey-high walls are located, precisely defining the external spaces. One of them is located on the entrance side, which faces a neighboring building and is almost completely solid, the other is on the garden side, where the "second face" of the house opens up towards the south-west and a crook by means of large openings. This courtyard is not hermetically enclosed, as for instance an inner-facing atrium, which captures the views, but it provides a finely weighted balance of sight-screen on the one hand and a view towards the surroundigs on the other. This ambivalence between enclosure and opening, between introvert and extrovert, creates a soft, gradual transition from the inside to the outside. In addition, it makes the contrast between the bare, new building and the luscious, old stock of trees a more gentle one.

Als Rückzugsort, als stilles Refugium zum Wohnen und Arbeiten dient ein Haus im Münsterland seinen Besitzern. Entsprechend ruhig und zurückhaltend gestalteten es die Architekten; die spröden Materialien und der rigide Minimalismus sind für ein Einfamilienwohnhaus außergewöhnlich. Stahlrahmen schneiden messerscharfe Öffnungen in den rohen Beton der Fassade, deren nackte Wandflächen als Projektionsfläche für das Schattenspiel der Bäume dienen. Vor dem Gebäude liegen geschosshoch ummauerte Höfe, die präzise Außenräume definieren. Der eine Hof liegt an der Eingangsseite, die sich fast fensterlos der benachbarten Bebauung verschließt, der andere auf der Gartenseite, wo das „zweite Gesicht" des Hauses über großzügige Öffnungen nach Südwesten auf einen Bachlauf schaut. Er ist nicht hermetisch abgeschlossen wie etwa ein innen liegendes Atrium, das die Blicke einfängt, sondern bietet eine fein abgewogene Balance zwischen Sichtschutz einerseits und Aussicht andererseits. Diese Ambivalenz zwischen Begrenzung und Öffnung, zwischen Introvertiertheit und Offenheit schafft einen sanften, schrittweisen Übergang von innen nach außen. Zusätzlich mildert sie den Kontrast zwischen dem kargen Neubau und dem üppigen alten Baumbestand.

haus truffer | ipsach . switzerland

DESIGN: :mlzd

The house of family Truffer is located in the middle of the country-side and by the bank of Biel Lake, with a view of the Jura moun-tains. Therefore, it is surprising at first that the architects grouped the rooms around a courtyard, since this rather introverted lifestyle actually does not do justice to the magnificent environment. The building is, however, by no means hermetically sealed off; it only appears a little inaccessible on the way there. A wooden box rests on a deflected, concrete plinth, which incorporates rooms on the ground floor. On the entrance side, the plinth breaks up and se-cures access to the center of the house, with the gravel surface of the drive-way leading towards the inside and further into the central atrium. This forms the heart of the house, with all the living rooms and the kitchen oriented towards this space. Full-length windows, which are built without frames into the floor and ceiling, appear to try and suspend the separation of inside and outside. The courtyard is the starting point of an "architectural promenade", since a ramp starts here in the direction of a roof terrace and makes it possible for the residents to explore the building as if on a showground. The bedrooms are located upstairs and open out onto the countryside by means of a glass façade, which is the height of a single storey.

Mitten im Grünen, nahe dem Ufer des Bielersees und mit Blick auf die Juraberge liegt das Haus der Familie Truffer. Daher ver-wundert es zunächst, dass die Architekten die Räume um einen Hof gruppierten, denn diese eher introvertierte Wohnform wird der herrlichen Umgebung eigentlich nicht gerecht. Das Gebäude schottet sich jedoch keineswegs hermetisch ab, lediglich in Rich-tung der Zufahrt gibt es sich ein wenig zugeknöpft. Auf einem abweisenden Betonsockel, der die Erdgeschossräume aufnimmt, ruht eine Holzbox. Auf der Eingangsseite reißt der Sockel auf und gewährt Zugang zur Hausmitte, der Kiesbelag der Zufahrt führt nach innen weiter in das zentrale Atrium. Dieses bildet das Herz-stück des Hauses, sämtliche Wohnräume und die Küche orientieren sich hierher. Raumhohe Fenster, am Boden und an der Decke rahmenlos eingebaut, scheinen die Grenze zwischen innen und außen aufheben zu wollen. Der Hof ist Ausgangspunkt einer „pro-menade architecturale", denn hier startet eine Rampe in Richtung Dachterrasse und ermöglicht den Bewohnern, das Gebäude einem Parcours gleich zu beschreiten. Oben liegen die Schlafräume, die sich über eine geschosshohe Glasfassade zur Landschaft öffnen.

Obergeschoss

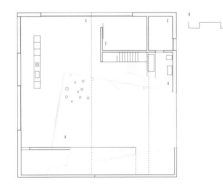

Legende:

0 Vorplatz
1 Wohnen/Essen
2 Keller
3 Gäste
4 Du/Wc
5 Zimmer
6 Zimmer
7 Spiel
8 Terrasse

Erdgeschoss

haus maria de la salut | maria de la salut . spain
DESIGN: Architekt Alexander Eduard Serda

Almond trees influence the image of the landscape in the north eastern part of Mallorca. 200 examples stand on the plot of a villa, near to the village of Maria de la Salut. By means of two atria, the building seeks a connection to the landscape. One of the atria is in the south and intended for common use, such as celebrating with guests at a party, while the other, northerly situated atrium serves the owner as a peaceful sanctuary. The pool has a special function: it penetrates the boundary wall of the courtyard and connects it with the neighboring environment. When the wooden gate is opened over the pool, the residents can swim through the wall towards the countryside. Sandstone slabs and teak-decking frame the water surface, which transports the multi-faceted light qualities into the house's interior by means of its reflections and—quite simply and purpose-driven—improves the micro-climate on summer days.

Mandelbäume prägen das Landschaftsbild im Nordosten Mallorcas. 200 Exemplare stehen auf dem Grundstück einer Villa nahe dem Dorf Maria de la Salut. Das Gebäude sucht über zwei Atrien den Bezug zur Landschaft, von denen das eine im Süden liegt und für gemeinschaftliche Benutzung vorgesehen ist, etwa wenn mit Gästen ein Fest gefeiert wird, während das andere, nördlich gelegene dem Hausherrn als stiller Rückzugsbereich dient. Eine besondere Funktion kommt dem Wasserbecken zu: Es durchstößt die Umfassungsmauer des Hofes und verbindet ihn mit der Umgebung. Wenn das Holztor über dem Becken geöffnet wird, können die Bewohner durch die Wand hindurch der Landschaft entgegenschwimmen. Sandsteinplatten und ein Teakholzdeck rahmen die Wasserfläche ein, die mit ihren Reflexionen die vielfältigen Lichtstimmungen ins Innere des Hauses transportiert und – ganz nüchtern und zweckorientiert – an heißen Sommertagen das Mikroklima verbessert.

villa neuendorf | mallorca . spain

DESIGN: Claudio Silvestrin

The dialogue between building and landscape is the central theme of a villa in the south of Mallorca. Like a medieval castle it overlooks the spacious site with such a natural air as if it had always been there. Since the architect had earth pigment from this area worked into the plaster, its mainly closed walls are in the same brownish color as the dry earth of the surrounding environment. A dead-straight narrow path, which is paved with natural stone typical for the region, leads over a stretch of one hundred meters up the slightly rising site towards the building, where a vertical slit just 83 centimeters wide dramatically cuts through the façade and provides access to the interior. Via this loophole, the visitor enters a courtyard. Whereas as he approached, he was still wondering how many rooms might be included in the imposing villa, now it turns out that the largest part is occupied by a quadratic, external room, which is embodied in the building volume. It measures 12 by 12 meters and is certainly not overfurnished—only a bench, made of local stone, invites the guest to sit down. On one of the remaining facades of the villa there is a pool that is directly joined to the building and, as a horizontal element like the path, merges the villa with its surroundings.

Der Dialog zwischen Gebäude und Landschaft ist das zentrale Thema einer Villa im Süden Mallorcas. Wie eine mittelalterliche Burg thront sie auf dem weitläufigen Grundstück mit einer Selbstverständlichkeit, als habe sie schon immer dort gestanden. Ihre weitgehend geschlossenen Mauern tragen die gleiche bräunliche Farbe wie der trockene Boden des Umlands, denn in den Putz ließ der Architekt Erdpigmente aus der Umgebung einarbeiten. Ein schmaler Pfad, der mit ortstypischem Naturstein gepflastert ist, führt über eine Strecke von hundert Metern kerzengerade das leicht ansteigende Gelände empor zum Gebäude, wo ein vertikaler Schlitz von nur 83 Zentimetern Breite die Fassade theatralisch durchschneidet und Zugang ins Innere gewährt. Durch diese „Schießscharte" betritt der Besucher einen Hof. Fragte er sich beim Herannahen noch, wie viele Räume die imposante Villa wohl beherberge, stellt sich nun heraus, dass ihr größter Teil von einem quadratischen Außenraum eingenommen wird, der dem Gebäudevolumen einverleibt ist. Er misst 12 mal 12 Meter und ist wahrlich nicht übermöbliert – lediglich eine Bank, aus einem Stein der Umgebung gefertigt, lädt zum Sitzen ein. Auf der anderen Seite des Gebäudes geht es in den Pool, der sich direkt an die Villa anschließt und sie ähnlich wie der Pfad als horizontales Element mit der Umgebung verzahnt.

index & photo credits

imprint

Bibliographic Information published by Die Deutsche Bibliothek
Die Deutsche Bibliothek lists this publication in the Deutsche
Nationalbibliografie; detailed bibliographic data are available in the
internet at http://dnb.ddb.de

ISBN 3-89986-050-0

1st edition

Printed in Austria

Editors | Martin Nicholas Kunz, Christian Schönwetter
Texts (page) | Christian Schönwetter (4, 10, 12, 14, 18, 22,
30, 36, 40, 48, 52, 60, 62, 76, 94, 96, 122, 134, 136, 144,
152, 156, 162, 164), Hartmut Möller (24, 32, 38, 58, 68, 70,
72, 82, 88, 92, 104, 110, 112, 114, 116, 126, 140, 148)
Translations | SAW Communications, Sabine A. Werner
Art Direction & Production | Markus Mutz
Digital Imaging | Jan Hausberg
Printing | Vorarlberger Verlagsanstalt AG, Dornbirn, Austria

Special thanks to: Lea Bauer, Hanna Martin

avedition GmbH
Königsallee 57 | 71638 Ludwigsburg | Germany
p +49-7141-1477391 | f +49-7141-1477399
www.avedition.com | kontakt@avedition.com

Martin Nicholas Kunz

1957 born in Hollywood.
Founder of fusion publishing
creating content for architecture, design, travel and
lifestyle publications.

Christian Schönwetter

1972 born in Bernkastel.
Studies of architecture at
the University of Karlsruhe,
Germany.
Journalist publishing books
and essays on architecture,
design and engineering for
German print and online
magazines.

best designed hotels:
Asia Pacific
Americas
Europe I (urban)
Europe II (countryside)
Swiss Hotels
Hotel Pools

best designed
wellness hotels:
Asia Pacific
Americas
Europe
Africa & Middle East

All books are released in
German and English